Help I've got a kid!

A survival guide for parents

Wayne R. Bartz PhD
and Richard A. Razor EdD
Strip cartoons by Dick Pike
Other illustrations by David Lock

⧉EXLEY

DEDICATION

To our parents, who endured our behaviour, and also to Jenell, Brad, Jennifer, Brian, Neil, Tricia, and Shannon, children close to us who challenged our wits and provided some of the examples for this book.

ACKNOWLEDGEMENTS

No book is ever solely the product of its authors. Many people lend their experience and expertise. *Help! I've Got a Kid!* is no different. We are indebted to Gerry Patterson for much of this book's research foundation, to Bob Alberti for his careful editing, Alden Paine for his helpful reviews, Mark Ackerman for his insightful evaluation and suggestions, and Carolyn Larsen who typed the manuscript from a frightful rough draft. Our appreciation is also extended to Dick Pike, the creative artist who did all the illustrations. Finally, a word of thanks is given to those closest to us who endured the many time demands and inconveniences of our writing task.

WRB and RAR

Published in Great Britain in 1987 by Exley Publications Ltd, 16 Chalk Hill, Watford, Herts WD1 4BN, United Kingdom in association with Impact Publishers.
Reprinted March 1989

© 1978 by Wayne R. Bartz and Richard A. Razor
© this British edition 1987 by Wayne R. Bartz and Richard A. Razor

British Library Cataloguing in Publication Data

Bartz, Wayne R.
  Help. I've got a kid.
  1. Child rearing.
  2. Behaviour modification.
  I. Title.
  II. Surviving with kids. *English*
  649'.64   HQ772

ISBN 1-85015-090-7 (Hbk)
ISBN 1-85015-182-2 (Pbk)

Typeset by Brush Off Studios, St Albans, Herts.
Printed and bound in Hungary.

The influence that parents can have on the lives of their children over a period of fifteen to eighteen years is incredible... Whether parents are aware of it or not, through their daily life styles and the consistency of their behaviour they teach their children how to blend, for better or worse, the basic ingredients for living – how to deal with anxiety, failure, how to handle money, make friends, be a friend, how to resolve conflicts and make decisions, how to live and how to be loved...

Research is telling us that healthy, balanced children who value themselves and others are likely to come from homes in which the parents respect and care for the children, each other, and themselves; where there are firm rules which are consistently enforced; and where there are high standards for behaviour and performance which children are expected to live up to.

Don E Hamachek
ENCOUNTERS WITH THE SELF

Contents

Introduction

Imagine yourself to be an overwhelmed parent with a couple of very active young children. Their behaviour often seems a catalogue of pure frustration:

★ They make lots of noise that often is ear-piercing.
★ They make a mess of practically everything they touch.
★ They 'can't find' toys, shoes, pencils, bikes, socks, pillows or clothes (and neither can you half the time!)
★ They often won't eat what's good for them unless you insist upon it. Then they act as if you are trying to poison them.
★ They manage to undo a clean house in two minutes.
★ The child's room itself is usually a disaster area.
★ They move at a snail's pace (or disappear entirely) when there is work to be done.
★ They are always running when you want them to walk or stand still. If you are in a hurry, they are 'too tired' to run. You begin to feel older than your years.
★ They mysteriously make your favourite things disappear.
★ They not only bring out the best in you – but the worst as well. You dream about when they will grow up.
★ They delight in pestering you while you're busy. Your anger worries you. Alcohol or tranquilisers don't help!

Happily, at times they also

★ run up to you and offer a warm hug when you meet them at school;
★ look across the room while playing and say 'I love you, Mummy';
★ win a football game, or bring home a prize from a school sports race;
★ make the honour roll at school;
★ pick a bouquet of fresh flowers for Mother's Day;
★ collect £20 for a charity.

The whole experience of relating to and raising children can be together exhausting and delightful. Yet there are many things along the way that can be done to reduce the exhaustion and increase the delight. That's why we wrote this book.

It is designed to be a practical aid to people who want to improve their relationships with children. It is based upon a large collection of evidence which shows that child behaviour can be changed. The main focus is on pre-teenagers but the principles are applicable to people of any age. We believe that children do not have a particularly 'good' or 'bad' nature, nor are they instinctively 'naughty', 'lazy', or 'insecure'. Their behaviour is overwhelmingly a product of learning. Although genetic inheritance may set broad limits upon our capabilities, it is really *learning* that determines how we behave, within those limits. Children often do not behave as parents want – but not *because* they are 'naughty' or 'bad'. These are labels given as a *result* of behaviour. The way to change the behaviour is for child and parent to learn better ways of dealing with the immediate living situation.

It has been traditional to explain children's behaviour in just the opposite way. For example, a frequent reason given for children doing poorly at school is that they simply have a negative attitude or are poorly motivated. The logical solution would then be to try to change the 'negative attitude'. But we don't believe that trying to change an *attitude* is what will lead to most success. Rather, it is being successful at school that will change the attitude! The school must arrange conditions which give the opportunity to succeed. Only then will a child begin to like the school experience. Similarly, a parent must arrange home life conditions which will encourage a child to succeed. It is too much to expect any child to feel suddenly confident and positive about anything before experiencing success at it. We must stress, of course, that each child is an individual and will not necessarily respond in a given situation the same way as another child. Any successful application of psychological principles clearly must be tailored to the person involved.

This book is about *relationships*. We recognise that relationships are held together by good feelings, and good feelings come from the positive things people do for one another. So this book naturally revolves around ways of doing nice things that make people feel good, and reduces the need for doing things that make people feel unhappy. That's what relating is all about!

Hopefully this book avoids most of the complicated jargon that psychologists and psychiatrists so often use, which was hard work for us! The extensive illustrations help to demonstrate principles, because we believe that 'one picture is worth a thousand words'. We selected our examples from our own lives and hundreds of situations suggested to us by students and parents. Many of the examples should be familiar and may even bring back memories from your own childhood. These selected examples cannot cover every problem a parent has to face. But, with a little imagination, the thirty principles demonstrated should be useful over a broad range of life situations. Our examples reflect values held by the parents portrayed in the cartoons. You may have different ideas about behaviour you desire in your children. However, the principles apply regardless of the behaviour involved.

We also believe that people should be parents by choice, with a conscious commitment to the tasks involved in responsible parenthood. This means they not only have a *right* to guide the behaviour of their children, but a *responsibility* to do so. Active guidance is quite different from the approach which assumes that children need only 'unconditional love' to blossom into healthy, happy adults. Constructive guidance and 'limit setting' can be applied with love, and are a realistic preparation for adult life. The world seldom offers permissive, unconditional 'love'! The active guidance we advocate is also very different from the heavy-handed approach of 'children should be seen and not heard'. We encourage parents to be 'lovingly firm'.

We are all greatly influenced throughout our lives – first by parents, then by teachers, friends, television, government, bosses, spouses, and many others who come into the act. Parents *do* influence their children, probably more than anyone else. They have, as part of their parental responsibility, the right to help their children learn to behave in ways they consider appropriate. At the same time, they have a responsibility to provide a warm and loving relationship that will foster a positive self concept and help each child to reach his or her potential. Sometimes these two goals seem to be in conflict, and the decisions are difficult.

We don't pretend that this book gives 'all the answers'. No book can. What we offer you here is a set of general principles, tested and proved with thousands of parents and children. Used consistently, they will work for *nearly* all parents with *nearly* all children. Nevertheless YOU AND YOUR CHILDREN ARE UNIQUE, and you must decide for yourself how to apply what you learn here.

In order to make such decisions wisely, we suggest you follow a procedure such as the following:

1. Read the entire book carefully.
2. Study principles you are not sure of;
3. Select one or two (no more at first!) areas on which you wish to work with your child;
4. Consider the goals you wish to achieve, the potential outcomes of this approach, and its limitations;
5. If you decide to go ahead, give your choice a chance! It will take some time, and perhaps some *additional* (temporary) problems will occur.
6. Evaluate success or failure in terms of your original goals. Remember that if you try to help your child to learn to express feelings, for example, and then you get upset when the child 'talks back' to you, that you have been 'successful', in terms of your original goal. ('OK, clever psychologist, so now what do I do?') The point here is to be careful to establish goals which you – and hopefully your child – really want to accomplish!

Parents have to make hundreds – if not thousands – of choices and decisions about their children's behaviour, and must consider the limits accepted by our society. Being a successful parent of a happy child is a rewarding experience, but also very hard work! We hope this book will make that work a bit easier.

Chapter One

Looking at Behaviour

'You're aggressive!'

'He's insecure.'

'She's intelligent.'

'He's paranoid!'

How often have you found yourself using such expressions? We all use labels for people in our daily lives, because they help us to classify, sort, and put order into our world, making it easier to understand. One may describe a neighbour as 'friendly', a business acquaintance as 'ambitious', and a relative or child as an 'extrovert'. This form of labelling helps us get a quick picture of what the person might be like, although we are aware (hopefully!) that it is a limited picture. We don't expect a *positive* label to tell us a great deal about the individual person, since labels are so general (there are many types of people we might call an 'extrovert'). Ironically, with undesirable behaviour we sometimes apply a descriptive label and then expect that label to *explain* the behaviour.

You have undoubtedly seen highly energetic children who sometimes wear parents down (maybe your own children at times)? Their attention span may be short, their interests endless, and they can be 'wound up' day and night. Thousands of such children have been labelled 'hyperactive' and treated by doctors with drugs, a practice that is now being seriously questioned. The label 'hyperactive', originally a name for certain behaviour, came to be seen as an *explanation* in itself.

Such thinking is dangerous. Johnny is full of energy and runs around a lot. We call that 'hyperactive'. *Why* does he run around a lot? *Because he's hyperactive. How* do we know he is hyperactive? *Because he runs around a lot!* Johnny's 'diagnos-

Labels, labels, labels

tic label' merely describes what he is like – it does not explain what causes his behaviour.

Do labels really tell us anything about a child? Norman's mother Martha made such excessive use of labels that we could also apply a label to her efforts as well: 'overkill!' While Norman was behaving badly, Martha indulged herself in the luxury of using labels as if they explained his behaviour. Finally, neighbour Marge used a few choice labels herself!

Look again at what Martha and Marge said. Do the labels aggressive, hyperactive, artistic, rebellious, brainwashed, silly, head-shrinker, or brat tell you anything useful about what actually happened in this situation? Do the labels really tell why? Indeed, you may consider Norman to be a 'brat', but his inexcusable behaviour is not caused by 'naughtiness'. It is maintained by its consequences, including his mother's inaction. Clearly, labels can lead parents into a blind alley because if labels *caused* troublesome behaviour, then parents couldn't do anything to change their children's actions. Fortunately, this isn't the case.

**Principle 1: Labels – such as 'hyperactive',
'aggressive' or 'insecure' – really don't
explain behaviour, nor do they give parents
guidance in how to deal with their children.**

Some difficult child behaviour may have its basis 'inside the child' – perhaps a result of body chemistry. Indeed, research is still being conducted to determine if some overactive children could be stimulated by the foods or chemical additives they eat. However, labels have been badly misused. For years we have labelled some people as 'retarded'. Expecting very little from such people, what did we get? That's right – very little. Schools, doctors and parents have overused labels such as underachiever, culturally deprived, emotionally disturbed, insecure and educationally handicapped. The result of all this labelling was often that teachers, hospitals, and even parents gave little meaningful help if a child was categorised as 'retarded' or 'disturbed'.

Labels will always be around, but why use them in ways

which incorrectly suggest there is little hope for change? Instead, we suggest that you avoid labels and ask instead:

'What is going on here?'
'What possible reasons could there be for the child to act this way?'
'Could I be accidentally encouraging this kind of behaviour because of *my* actions?'

Starting to look for influences within the environment rather than within the individual child is the first step in understanding behaviour.

Imagine that Grandma, Grandpa, and a proud new father are in the maternity ward looking through the window at a newborn boy. Grandma beams to her son 'He's lovely! He certainly looks a lot like you.'

The new father replies 'Yes, he does look a lot like me, but he has his mother's hair.'

Grandpa says, 'Oh, I don't know. I think he has his mother's forehead, though...One thing is certain, he's got the Johnson chin!'

We've all heard such conversations. It's fun to look at a newborn and try to spot family characteristics. We also try to be rather 'democratic' about it in making sure that at least one physical characteristic is attributed to each member of the immediate family. Actually, a day-old baby probably doesn't show much in the way of resemblance to anybody. Later on, as physical features become more evident, we may begin to see some likeness between the young child and parents or grandparents. If the son develops 'frizzy' hair, and the only person in the family who has hair like that is Grandpa on Dad's side, we are on fairly safe ground to assume that the frizzy hair came from Grandpa. Indeed, most of our physical characteristics are inherited.

Many people think of behaviour as a collection of personality traits that are also inherited from parents and grandparents, much like eye colour or hair texture. The best evidence available suggests that, while the *foundations* for behaviour are inherited, most behaviour is learned through life experiences.

Principle 2: Behaviour is influenced by two major factors: heredity and learning.

We do not believe that genetics provides an adequate explanation for specific behaviour. Children do inherit physical traits and a certain biochemical make-up, which may help or hinder them in various activities. All of these forces, however, interact with what the child learns from life experiences.

Inherited physical structure increases the chances for various types of behaviour. For example, a child who has inherited a strong and sturdy body is more likely to be involved in and successful at sports. A youngster who is attractive is more likely to be outgoing and involved socially. The child who inherits a highly developed brain has the potential to excel in intellectual activities.

The point is, we don't inherit behaviour! What we do in-

The 'inherited' temper

herit is a broad potential to behave in a million different ways. We don't inherit bad temper, stubbornness, laziness, or violent aggressiveness. Nor, on the positive side, do we inherit industriousness, friendliness, leadership, courage, or honesty. All of these characteristics and values (often assumed to be characteristics of different social or national groups) are the result of different *learning* experiences, rather than heredity.

Learning to share your toys is a hard lesson, and it's a rare young child who willingly gives up prized possessions to let another use them, even for a few minutes. In the illustration, Mum suggests that Jimmy's temper is a 'personality trait' unique to Dad's O'Grady family and Irish origins. But is the temper really something *inside* Jimmy? Actually, anger in such situations is common to children everywhere, and is learned, not inherited. Even very young children see that the expression of anger sometimes achieves goals.

For parents, the fact that behaviour is determined by learning is actually a great blessing. If all behaviour was inherited, we would be stuck with a trait like the 'O'Grady temper', and never would be able to change it! No parent can change a child's genetic structure. Parents can and do have a tremendous effect upon their children through learning. (We don't want to give the impression that parents exclusively determine a child's behaviour, however. All sorts of people are involved. Also, children certainly influence parents!) We'll examine this complex-yet-simple learning process in detail in the rest of the book.

Chapter Two

Why do Children Act the Way They Do?

Have you ever known parents who think their child is an 'angel', while you are convinced the child is a 'monster'? We do not always agree on what is 'good' or 'bad' behaviour in children. This is also true among nations, cultures, or socio-economic groups. Actions considered 'good' in a Northern European country, for instance, may be considered 'bad' in the Middle East. Also our judgement changes over time: many characteristics considered 'unacceptable' for women in the early part of this century, such as assertiveness, are considered desirable today. What is acceptable and what is unacceptable is a matter of opinion, but all behaviour is *acquired* in the same way, no mattter how we *label* it. Within your own family there is probably general agreement about what is acceptable and unacceptable behaviour.

Obviously, no one wants children to learn 'bad' habits! They often do, nonetheless, and parents can sometimes see where they got such habits, perhaps from friends, school, television, or even other family members! Sometimes it seems a mystery: how did the child ever pick that up? Why does it continue in the face of punishment? In such cases, parents may be *accidentally teaching* the behaviour and helping to maintain it by their reactions to it!

To illustrate, let us look at examples of children being

'Help, I'm hurt!'

taught to run to their mother in two entirely different situations. In the first cartoon example, Mother paid attention to a crying child who may have been injured. Upon closer inspection, it was clear that Freddie had not hurt himself seriously, so Mother showed him how to deal with it and sent him on his way. Clearly she was interested in and concerned about his welfare. Most mothers would want a small child to come to them immediately when there is any possibility of physical injury. By her warm response, Mother encourages and teaches Freddie to come to her when he is *hurt*. He learns that Mother gives help and comfort when he needs them.

In the second set of cartoons, Mother paid attention to Billy's crying over an argument with his older brother. By her warm response, and by telling Timmy to share the trolley she

---

Principle 3: Most human behaviour is learned. Children learn both desirable and undesirable behaviour in the same way.

'Help, I didn't get my way!'

is encouraging and teaching her son to cry and run to her when he does not *get his own way*. Billy learns that Mother will help him get his own way with other children. Most mothers do not want a child to run crying to them over every disagreement or upset. Note that in both cases the behaviour is being learned in *exactly* the same way, whether the parent wants it or not.

In the first case, if we asked his mother why Freddie runs crying to her when hurt, she would see nothing surprising about it. 'Why, I want him to do that. I fix his little hurts, and make him feel better,' she might say.

In the second example, if asked why Billy runs crying to her every time he does not get his own way in a dispute with his brother, his mother might be truly mystified, and say something like, 'I don't know. I just can't understand it. I tell him to try to get along with his brother, and I make his brother play with him, but he just keeps on crying, and running to me every time they argue.'

Mother isn't trying to teach her children to do things that bother her (and which are not in their own best interests), but nevertheless she is doing just that, by paying attention to the very behaviour she might not want. Instead, she could have told the boys to work it out themselves. Other undesirable behaviour is learned in much the same way: acting defiantly; hurting others; truancy; stealing. The people who do such things have systematically – even if unintentionally – been taught to behave in ways society considers undesirable.

Please understand that we do not wish to discourage mothers from comforting their children when they are hurt! On the contrary! The point of this discussion is that touching,

Pity the poor substitute teacher

24

hugging, and attention from loved ones are powerful means of strengthening specific behaviours. Thus parents need to be aware of the effect of their responses to their children, and that they are teachers of child behaviour – even if by accident!

The main point we would like you to remember is that *your child's behaviour*, whether appropriate or inappropriate, *is learned*. The principles involved in that learning are the subject of this book.

Every now and then we encounter parents who are surprised to find out that their child is quiet, co-operative, and perhaps even docile at school. At home, they find the child loud, negative, and almost constantly in trouble. Such parents may see nothing unusual in the observation that their own behaviour is very different at home, at work, with friends, or while on holiday. Why not their children as well? We all direct our actions to what is expected by the situation.

Principle 4: All people, including children, behave differently depending on where they are and who they are with.

Children, like adults, learn what behaviour fits what situations, so that places, people, and events become 'cues' for both desirable and undesirable behaviour.

Like a green light that has been turned on, the class goes wild when the substitute teacher shows up. The students are well aware that Mrs Praether doesn't know them, can have little effect on their marks, and probably will not be seen again for the rest of the year. So why work? Why not play or just do nothing, or even enjoy tormenting her? The substitute becomes a 'cue' for acting up. When the regular teacher returns, she finds it hard to believe that her normally well-behaved group could possibly have been so unruly.

The immediate effect of cues upon behaviour can be seen in a variety of situations. For example, some young children cry when parents are about to go out and leave them with a babysitter. Yet the minute the door closes, the crying stops. Some brothers and sisters will fight noisily when parents are around, yet play well together when alone. Children can also behave ideally at home but cause perpetual problems at school. Situations, people, and places serve as *cues* for all sorts of behaviour.

Richard Rasor remembers when, as a child, he rarely cried when hurt – that is, until he saw his mother. Then tears would burst forth. In this instance, the sight of his mother was the only additional cue he needed to put forth a great show of pain – comforting would soon follow.

Our point is this: children's actions make sense in terms of the situation. Sometimes the cues are very subtle and not noticed. In other cases, they are obvious. When we look at the complexities of each unique individual, and the variety of situations which occur in our lives, it is not difficult to see why behaviour can at times seem to be beyond explanation!

Chapter Three

Everybody Likes to Feel Good

If somebody suggested that your life revolved around a system of reward and punishments, would you agree? As you might have guessed, we would! A reward, as we view it, can actually be almost anything, depending upon individual preferences ranging from hugs, compliments, or self-congratulations on a job well done, to the more material things like sweets, gold stars, or money. Whatever it may be, if it represents a good result, it will tend to increase the behaviour it follows. If you say 'Hello!' to someone in the morning and that person nods and smiles back, you will be more likely to say 'Hello!' again the next day (assuming you value nods and smiles). However, if you receive a sneer or snub in response, you will probably stop greeting that person.

**Principle 5: We keep doing things which
bring good results or good feelings
(rewards).**

**Principle 6: We stop doing things which
bring bad results, or bad feelings
(no rewards).**

Encouraging children to talk to parents

These principles seem so basic and such common sense that they may appear hardly worthy of mention. Yet they are of profound importance, and are misused daily by parents, schools, government, and business. For example, where is the incentive for a child to keep doing chores if the effort goes unnoticed? Why would a child try hard in school if every attempt earns poor marks and/or parental scorn? Where is the reward, in a 'planned obsolescence economy', for a manufacturer to produce an economical car that will last twenty years?

It is easy to see, and even 'understand' the basic reward and

Discouraging children from talking to parents

punishment principles, but successful application is not so easy. In fact, most of the thirty principles in this book are directed toward different aspects of the effective use of rewards with children.

Consider the above two examples involving conversation between an adult and a child. When Susan said, 'Look what I made in school today,' her invitation was followed by good reactions: Mother looked pleased and said something positive. When Susan asked if her mother wanted to know more, she was encouraged to talk about her achievement. By her interest and attention, her mother has actually 'rewarded' showing and talking about the project. Because of her mother's warm actions, we can expect that Susan will continue to talk to her mother about school and probably about other things as well.

In our next example, another mother does something different. This mother also gave her daughter attention and a smile for showing what she made at school, but here the similarity ends. In this case, Mother really *discouraged* any talk about the child's achievement, and Carol can assume that her mother wasn't interested and wanted her to go to her room. In effect, Carol was *punished* for trying to tell her mother about her achievement. If this were to happen very often, we can predict with some certainty that the child will seldom try to start conversations with her mother in the future.

We have all seen children who are outgoing, talkative, and who seem to enjoy conversing with adults. In contrast, we also have seen children whom we might call 'shy' or even 'withdrawn' – children who don't say much and who will answer a question with very few words, or may not even answer at all. It appears that some children have been taught to be outgoing and others to be shy through a system – intentional or unintentional – of rewards, or lack of them.

We are not saying that parents must always instantly stop whatever they are doing and pay attention to a child who has interrupted! That is a good way to teach the child to interrupt! However, parents who intentionally wish to encourage behaviour they like must make an attempt to reward it, and that may mean making an extra effort. In our example, it may mean listening to explanations and 'child or baby talk' that is frankly not very interesting to an adult.

Nevertheless, the long-term benefits to the child – particularly in the area of human relationships – will also be of value to the parents.

Another common example: children often learn not to talk about sex to their parents. Youngsters are not encouraged to express their curiosity, or may even be actively discouraged and socially punished, forcing them to get their sex education elsewhere. While most people agree that sex education should come from parents, few parents actually encourage their children to ask questions about sex in a direct, honest manner.

We have given simple examples here of reward and punishment. More complex examples will follow in later chapters. The reward principle is the foundation of most of what is known about human behaviour. It applies to all behaviour, all people, and all ages. It is as true when dealing with yourself as it is with others. *If you want a type of behaviour to continue, reward it.* If it is not rewarded in some way, at least sometimes, it will not continue.

Nearly all living creatures are attracted to situations that make them feel good and are put off by painful events. We humans, the most complex of living things, are strongly influenced by our various emotions. Depending on our personal experiences, particular people or places become *associated* with good or bad feelings. Such feelings may persist years later.

Try to recreate some of your own childhood experiences and feelings. Sit back, close your eyes, relax, and breathe deeply. Think of a very close person from your childhood, such as your father, mother, or a friend. Imagine you are with this person, reliving an experience from your childhood. Spend three or four minutes with your imagination and note any changes in bodily feelings. Go ahead and do it now...

If you were really able to create a vivid memory, you may have experienced strong feelings or emotions, some positive and maybe some negative. If childhood experiences are predominantly pleasant, a child will grow to adulthood having good feelings associated with those experiences – with parents, school, and friends. But, if a child is continuously treated badly within the family or by other adults, he or she may grow up feeling uncomfortable and perhaps even hostile or resentful around those persons (or even adults in general). It is not surprising that such children react against parental figures. We can acquire such feelings at any time of life.

Principle 7: Our learning experiences determine when we feel such natural emotions as love, elation, anxiety, and sadness.

If a very young boy is smacked or otherwise hurt several times while in the presence of a nice, furry white rabbit, we will find that he begins to show signs of alarm at the mere sight of the rabbit. On the other hand, if he receives hugs and smiles when he is with the rabbit, he will begin to feel good when he sees the animal. Such feelings can last months, years, or even a lifetime, unless he has an experience which modifies this learning.

Learning to feel good about someone

This process of learning by association is known more formally as 'classical conditioning'. It tells us simply that objects or events which are grouped together in time, place, or situation often tend to be associated, and therefore call up the same feelings. We develop fear of, or fondness for anything as a result of what it has been 'associated' with in our early learning experiences. Seeing blood, for example, may lead to crying, if the sight of blood is repeatedly associated with pain. Given enough such associations of blood with pain, the sight of blood alone can generate fear and crying, even when physical pain is absent. Similarly, if good feelings, smiles, and loving are regularly associated with a particular person, just the thought of that person will likely result in a 'warm glow'. Here are a couple of examples.

Uncle Stan is obviously a special person in Joey's life. When Uncle Stan came for visits, he helped Joey feel happy by doing enjoyable things with him that were appropriate for his age. So, later memories of Stan and his name produce good feelings.

Learning to feel badly about someone

A lifetime includes hundreds of people (teachers, aunts, uncles, parents, friends, brothers or sisters) who can bring back memories and emotions, pleasant or unpleasant. Ideally, in a family, mum and dad want to create situations, events, and relationships with children that produce good feelings for both parents and children. People who experience good feelings in their day-to-day lives also tend to have good feelings about themselves. The best way to teach children to value themselves and to be good parents someday, is to make their childhood happy.

Even the most well-intentioned efforts of adults don't automatically result in good feelings for children. Uncle Harold meant well, but he was rough and inflicted pain upon Billy every time he saw him. When continued over the years, Harold himself became a 'pain' and even his name produced bad feelings twenty years later.

It is easy to attach emotions to names. If you were trying to pick a name right now for a newborn son, which among the following would you be *least* likely to pick? And why?

Adolf	Dagwood
Percy	Charles
Richard	Zachariah

Since all names are originally neutral, upon what basis do we make a choice? It is because names take on meaning and produce feelings through association, some positive and some not so positive (perhaps some even sound ridiculous). There is nothing strange about how we come to feel good or bad about people, places, or events.

Chapter Four

Each Child is Unique

When we were children, many households had a ready supply of biscuits, lemonade or squash, which were often used as rewards (for doing jobs, keeping 'out from under foot', small successes at school or in sports). At that time, there was not the variety of 'children's treats' on the market which there is today. With a tremendous range of biscuits, sweets and cakes and drinks available now, a parent cannot assume that a biscuit will have the value for children that it did when we were young.

Obvious? Perhaps, but we have seen parents become astonished when a child rejected a 'reward' that was offered. The *parent* considered the item as a reward; the child's reaction demonstrated clearly that it was not!

> **Principle 8: Because each person is unique,
> rewards must also be unique – that is,
> 'tailor-made' to fit the individual.**

When Grandpa was a child, getting a penny from his parents or grandparents was a big treat and he remembers it vividly, so he assumes that his grandchildren will consider it a great reward.

A penny isn't what it used to be

It is simply an economic fact that today's penny is not worth much. When Grandpa was a youngster, it might have purchased a respectable amount of sweets. To these children his suggestion of a 'big surprise' evidently meant something else. Often bedtime is also a time of conflict since children don't like to get ready for bed and leave adult company. It is a rare young child who admits to being tired and wanting to go to bed! In this case the big surprise turned out to be no real surprise at all, leaving the children upset and perhaps feeling cheated, and Grandpa hurt and perplexed. His gesture of love was not seen by the children as generous, despite his caring intent.

This type of outcome happens in different ways at different ages. Parents sometimes offer 'dinner out' as a reward, having in mind a nice restaurant. But where do the children want to go? A pizza house or fast food place! Besides avoiding the assumption that children will like what parents like (or did like when they were children), we need to keep in mind the tastes of individual children.

The following illustration shows another example of the importance of making the reward fit the individual situation.

Going camping for the weekend may be exciting for Dad, and may have been for the kids when they were younger. But now dating and seeing friends have become very important. They may be more valued than spending the weekend with the family. So this 'reward' is actually only a reward for one of the children, and may even be thought a punishment by the

Teenage individuality

son who would miss the dance. Dad comes up with another reward, a traditionally 'masculine' outing like fishing, which Dad assumes will appeal to his son, while Mum does the same thing with her daughter, assuming that shopping and a visit to the hairdressers will appeal to her because she is female. Fortunately, in recent years such sex stereotypes have come seriously into question, so that now boys and girls can feel free to do many things which might have been denied them in the past because they were 'unmasculine' or 'unfeminine'. So if the parents in our illustration are aware of their children's *individual* needs and desires, the son will get his hair-do and the daughter her fishing trip. (Hopefully, the parents will also get some special time with their children!)

If parents are to be effective in the use of rewards, they need to do a lot of questioning, observing, and testing to find out who likes what. We just can't make assumptions about what others like. There is no universal reward for all people of all ages. As parents, we can't assume that children necessarily like what we like, that what one child likes will be liked by another, that children's preference will not change over time, or that the sex of the child will tell you what he or she might like. This point is summed up nicely in a recent popular slogan: 'Different strokes for different folks'.

When we talk about rewards and their use with children, a common reaction from parents is, 'Why, you're talking about a system of bribes!' This concern is expressed so often that we want to give it special attention.

Suggesting the use of rewards with children is nothing new – it is the *systematic, planned* use of rewards that is important. All of us spend our lives in a constantly changing system of rewards – from early parental hugs and affection to gold stars in school, and on to grade marks and certificates. As adults we have salary scales, promotions, status, as well as interpersonal rewards from relationships with family and friends. It seems when people express a concern about 'bribes' it is not the idea of *reward* that they are objecting to, but the specific use of money as a reward, or objects purchased with money. Note, however, that hardly anyone considers a salary from work to be a bribe, nor do parents think of weekly pocket-money for their children as a bribe. And it is ridiculous to think of a hug, or a smile, or other spontaneous expression of love as a bribe!

So 'bribe' is really a loaded word. To most people the word suggests some kind of shady deal, a payment for something that shouldn't really be done. 'Reward' and 'bribe' then, are not the same thing. A reward is a tangible expression of approval. A bribe is a payment for something 'illegal' or of questionable ethics.

With parents, this problem seems to come up most in situations where they assume the child 'should' do something because of 'duty' or self-motivation. In such situations parents often see any sort of reward as being unnecessary or excessive, especially if the child doesn't want to do something a parent thinks he or she should want to do. They may even feel that what the child really needs is a good smack. Yet we must remember that all of us do things because of the rewards involved – some immediate, some distant, some from ourselves, some from others. Children are no different.

We have heard parents protest, 'Well, once you start rewarding children they won't want to do anything without a reward. Are you going to follow them around the rest of their lives giving out rewards?' Of course not. We do not suddenly 'start' rewarding children. Their world is already full of rewards (and punishments). Parents can become *systematic*, however, by using those rewards which are preferred by individual children to motivate them toward desired behaviour.

A child who is not learning to read may dislike reading because of the experience of failure. The parent may think the child should 'want' to read. If nothing is done, the result is a non-reading child, who falls further behind. Instead, the parent or teacher can use some kind of simple reward, such as points, tokens, or gold stars, to get the child to start reading and to motivate practice. As the child succeeds, that reward will no longer be necessary because reading itself, and the wonderful horizons it offers, become rewarding. Nobody has to follow a reading child around for the rest of his or her life rewarding reading! However you may have to offer an extra incentive to the non-reader for those first attempts, in order to get that child started.

All parents are rewarded in a variety of ways for the things they do. Some of the ways are obvious (such as money or fame), and some are much harder to see but no less effective (self-congratulations or the respect of valued friends). These are not bribes for us, nor are our children's prized rewards bribes for them! Systematic rewards merely bring the natural learning process under a degree of control.

Principle 9: We all like material rewards such as money, food or toys. But it is really social rewards like attention, praise, and affection that make us feel good about ourselves.

What kinds of material rewards do you value? The list might include a nice home, clothes, jewellery, cars, perfume, boats – just about anything money will buy! Of course children have their prized rewards too: sweets, biscuits, dolls, toys. *Material* rewards (as we use the term) are tangible objects that have some economic value.

There is another very important type of reward – the *social* variety. Social rewards are intangible, cost nothing, and there is no limit to the supply. Some of the most important rewards for children are attention, praise, smiles, affection, touching and laughter. When it comes to social rewards, it is interesting to note that adults respond to the same things that children like. In fact, most of our adult interactions and relationships are based upon social rewards.

There are also a few rewards that seem to fit into both categories, material objects that have primarily social value, such as gold stars, points, or marks. For adults, status, position, titles, and maybe even medals, qualify.

Social rewards are far more important than material rewards in changing behaviour. We agree that most of us would like to have lots of material possessions! Wealth can indeed make life easier, but happiness and feelings of satisfaction with life depend upon a great deal more than just material wealth. Social interactions – that is human relationships – give life its warmth and vitality. No one ever gets tired of friendship, love, appreciation, concern, or interest from others!

Never underestimate the power of social rewards. Long-term change doesn't come about from sweets and biscuits or gold stars. Meaningful behaviour change comes from relating to children with love and care.

Let us look at two situations involving school reports and social rewards. In the first set of cartoons, Len's Dad rather mechanically gave him a material reward. He showed little interest and no real enthusiasm except for the cash. Certainly Len will enjoy the money, but the human social reward, so important between father and son, seemed to be missing.

Reaction to a school report

In the second cartoon (overleaf) we find a contrast: Dad responded with interest, showed pleasure in his facial expression, in touching his son, and in telling Rob how proud he was. He also gave him a material reward, but the situation is rich in social rewards. Rob will feel gratified, proud, and happy with this experience, which was certainly an improvement over the first businesslike transaction.

Another reaction to a school report

The use or non-use of money for school achievements is not really the issue here. Some parents feel happy about giving a 'bonus' for good marks, while others do not. The point is that, whether or not money is used, the *real reward* in terms of the parent-child relationship is the *social* reward. That is the one that will have the *greatest long-term effects*. We should note that the use of a material bonus for children's achievements is in no way different from what happens with many adults who get something special for a 'job well done'. Any kind of bonus is in part a social reward too, since it calls attention to the person's behaviour and singles it out for recognition. But, like the child example, a bonus paid to Dad or Mum by the boss personally, with a pat on the back and a comment about how good a job has been done, will certainly have more effect than just a cheque that shows up in a pay envelope without comment.

One final observation concerning the parent who fails to use social rewards. We sometimes hear young people say, 'My dad was OK I suppose but he didn't give anything of *himself.* Oh, he would give me money and buy me things, but there was no feeling between us.' Or from a father, 'After all I did for my son he still doesn't seem to respect me. I don't understand it. I bought him everything he wanted.' Obviously material rewards are not enough!

44

Chapter Five

Parents DO Have Influence!

Not long ago a worried mother said to us, 'I don't know why David is always under my feet. He just won't leave me alone for a moment. I try to get him to play by himself with interesting toys. I've told him to go into his room or to play with other children. I've even smacked him, but nothing seems to work. I don't know...this whole thing is probably due to the divorce, and now he's insecure.'

Indeed, a divorce may cause adjustment problems for people working out a new lifestyle, but the chances are David pesters his mother because she accidently rewards him, even though she wants him to stop. Her looks, touches, scolds, and even smacks are still attention to David. To help him through the divorce adjustment, his mother needs to give him lots of reassurance and attention – but carefully to avoid doing so at times when David is acting in undesirable ways.

Principle 10: Attention is one of the most powerful social rewards, for both desirable and undesirable behaviour. Even scolding a child is paying attention, and may be rewarding!

Attention maintaining an undesirable behaviour

Although it may seem obvious that attention can be a social reward, we want to emphasise not so much the obvious forms of attention (shouting, touching, grabbing), but the more subtle forms, such as a glance, smile, frown, eye contact, or physical gesture. In many families there is troublesome child behaviour that is maintained by exactly these types of subtle attention rewards.

If we were to question Susan's mother as to just what was going on in the illustration, she might tell us that she first tried explaining the situation to Susan, then asked her to go outside (repeated by Dad), and then suggested something else to capture Susan's interest. Indeed, those things happened. But what else was her mother doing? She was giving repeated attention to the very behaviour she wanted Susan to stop, thereby actually offering subtle encouragement to continue interrupting, asking questions, and staying in the room! Even Dad, by looking at Susan during these exchanges – however 'harshly' – gave an attention reward.

What else could these parents have done? How about simply ignoring the undesired behaviour? 'What,' you say, 'How could they just ignore it?' We're going to save a detailed answer to your question for Chapter 7. For now, the point is that the parents in this example are actively involved in teaching Susan behaviour through social rewards, despite the fact that it is the exact behaviour they did not want! To change the situation, they will have to change markedly their use of attention. It is a simple application of the principles of reward and attention: if children are getting the love and attention they need, and if they learn that they will not get them by remaining 'underfoot', by tantrums, or by interrupting adult conversations, such problems will diminish (in time, and with considerable patience)!

Many parents and teachers alike operate under the mistaken belief that publicly noticing 'bad behaviour' will somehow stop it (indeed, much of our society operates on this erroneous principle). 'Johnnie, Mother is watching.' 'Don't go in there!' 'Leave your brother alone!' 'Put that down this instant!' Imagine a teacher looking out at her class: 'Who is talking over there? Is that you, Peggy? Stop it right now! I expect to have absolute quiet in here.' Often children giggle when a teacher reacts like that. Or the teacher may say: 'Linda, get back in your seat. What are you doing on that side of the classroom?' Is the teacher's public notice going to stop the behaviour, or is it actually an *attention reward* for the child? Aren't the talkers and walkers in that classroom being actively rewarded by attention? Many studies have demonstrated that such attention produces more and more of the very behaviour that teachers want to end in their classrooms.

It is important to note, of course, that teachers and parents do not have control over *all* of the rewards (attention, in this example) which the child may receive in the situation. Disruptive classroom behaviour, for instance, is powerfully rewarded by the attention of other children. In such cases, it may be necessary to use other procedures to eliminate the behaviour.

We have heard a number of amusing examples in which college students purposely used attention in the classroom markedly to change their professor's behaviour without his or her knowledge of what was going on. One professor we knew tended to give very dull lectures, reading in a monotonous voice from his notes. Yet on rare occasions he would digress from the notes and describe interesting personal experiences related to the topic. Three students sitting in the front of the classroom agreed privately to look bored and

PARENTS 19,000 HOURS

TEACHERS 5,000 HOURS

TV 13,000 HOURS

OTHER CHILDREN 14,000 HOURS

Approximate number of hours spent
in presence of modelling influence (0-12 years)

inattentive during the lectures from notes, but to look very attentive and smile immediately when the professor talked about personal experiences. Within two weeks the professor, who did not know about the 'experiment', was not referring to his notes at all. Such is the power of attention and other social rewards!

'Monkey see, monkey do' was a popular saying among parents when we were children. The slogan didn't have much to do with monkeys but rather reflected a common observation of parents that children learn a great deal by just watching the behaviour of others. Author James Baldwin sums it up: 'Children have never been very good at listening to their elders, but they have never failed to imitate them.'

Principle 11: Much of our behaviour is learned by imitating the people around us, particularly parents.

This principle is probably no great surprise to anyone, yet parents sometimes forget that very alert eyes and ears are frequently tuned to them. Through the modelling process a child learns values, attitudes, gestures, vocabulary – and bad habits. Consider the simple ritual of eating. If a child spends an average of an hour a day eating with parents, that child has a daily opportunity to imitate them in the ways they eat, types of food eaten, tone of conversation, speed, food sequence. If you calculate the total number of those eating hours during the child's first twelve years, you will find that it amounts to 4,380 hours! Imagine how much a child must learn from parents after that many hours of observation! It's staggering when we consider the number of hours children actually spend observing and imitating the full range of adult behaviour.

Young adults often deny that they are like their parents. Certainly specific behaviour might be quite different. Yet psychologists have found that the best *single* indicator of what a person will be like as an adult is what the parents were like. For instance, grown children are likely to belong to the same political party as their parents, and to have similar religious beliefs. (Yes, we can think of exceptions too!)

During the growing years, children are exposed to a tremendous variety of 'models' they can imitate, including their parents. Playmates (particularly older and well-liked ones), school teachers, and heroes/heroines on TV, all serve as role models. It is really interesting to compare estimates of the total number of hours available (up to twelve years) to be influenced by those four categories of models.

Parents are clearly the most powerful childhood models, because they are such a dominant part of the young child's world. But the older children get, the stronger other influences become.

A Comment about TV

Research studies have shown that children readily imitate models who have high status and prestige and who are seen to be rewarded for what they do. Television personalities, superstars, and fantasy characters certainly have status, are often hero-worshipped by children, and are almost always rewarded for what they demonstrate on the screen.

There has been much debate and concern about television violence and its effects on children. We don't claim that watching a murder scene will necessarily cause an increase in the murder rate. It's not that simple. Yet the question must be raised: just what are we teaching children with television? Our time estimate allowed the average child three hours per day watching television, but we have seen estimates for American children as high as seven hours per day!

Nobody wants children to imitate television violence, yet according to one government study (US National Commission on the Causes and Prevention of Violence), during an average TV viewing week the programmes contained over 600 acts of violence. More than half the major characters (the models) inflicted violence on someone else. Violence also occurred in 95 per cent of the televised cartoons. Such violence is often caused by 'good guys' to 'bad guys' so it fits within our concepts of good versus evil. Can anyone realistically maintain that twelve years of exposure to this will have no adverse effect upon children? We doubt it. At the very least it makes us less sensitive to the pain and suffering of others. And at the worst....?

Chapter Six

'Too Much Love' Never Hurt Anybody

"The children now love luxury. They have bad manners, contempt for authority, they show disrespect to their elders...They no longer rise when elders enter the room. They contradict their parents, chatter before company, gobble up dainties at the table, cross their legs, and are tyrants over their teachers."

Does any of that sound familiar? It is attributed to the Greek philosopher Socrates some 2,000 years ago! No doubt parents of every generation have commented on the spoiling of youth. Let's take a look at this concern in some detail.

A 'spoiled child' usually gets his or her own way regardless of parental wishes. Sometimes they can be annoying or even downright objectionable. Still, some parents tolerate it and wonder why the problem behaviour continues. Such parents usually avoid any contradiction of the child's wishes and often give the impression that they want to be very popular with their children. Because they give many material and social rewards to children, it is only natural to wonder if it isn't the *rewards* that have spoiled the child. The fact of the matter is that the child has been *taught* to behave in an objectionable manner, not intentionally, but by being rewarded *for bad behaviour*.

53

Principle 12: Parents need not worry about giving 'too much' love and affection. The way to 'spoil' a child is to reward undesirable behaviour.

We want to point out that it is not an overabundance of rewards that results in a child behaving badly, but the non-systematic use of rewards. If a child is rewarded for all actions, we can expect to see a continuation of both good and bad behaviour.

The end result of years of this lifestyle is that the child's behaviour gets worse and worse until parents are so frustrated they don't know what to do. Some seek professional help. They feel love for their child, yet are frustrated by the child's behaviour. Such parents may be so constantly angry that they can scarcely contain their anger, perhaps saying, "I don't understand it, we've done everything for the boy, we've given him everything, we've loved him, and yet he's always in trouble. At times I could wring his neck!"

The key to understanding lies in looking at *how* a child is being rewarded.

Mother, by being nice and consoling, is hoping Cindy will change her mind and co-operate. Her idea may be that if she gives love when there is defiant behaviour there will no longer be a need to be defiant. She explains, and finally gives in, changing her shopping plans (and inconveniencing her friend) to fit Cindy's whim. While we might admire Mother's patience and her attempts to help her daughter understand the situation, she is nonetheless socially rewarding defiance with attention, touch, verbal warmth, concern in her voice, and giving in. If this sort of interaction continues, we can predict that Cindy will say 'No' even more often. Mother is demonstrating how to start 'spoiling' a child.

This mother, like most mothers, knows that children will be defiant now and then, and will test the limits of parental patience. But instead of stopping everything and socially rewarding defiance as in the first example, this mother pays minimal attention to it and doesn't let her daughter's 'no'

When the child says 'no' – socially rewarding defiance
interfere with plans. In effect, her mother is teaching Sally
that saying 'No' doesn't win – there is no reward for acting
defiantly. If her mother is consistent, Sally will try this tactic
less and less. Ideally, the mother might have planned not to
take her child shopping in the first place as children sometimes find such outings boring and tiresome. But, if the
situation (such as the one overleaf) demands that a child
comply with a reasonable request, the mother must 'stick to

When the child says 'no' – another approach

her guns' and insist upon compliance with a minimum of argument. Resistance to unwelcome tasks can often be avoided if a small treat for everybody is promised ahead of time, such as an ice cream cone or a few minutes of play at the park. (Caution: *Don't* make such an offer *following* an act of defiance!)

We are not suggesting here that children should ideally be like robots who unquestioningly jump and obey every parental command. Children have rights too, including the expression of their own desires and sometimes not wanting to participate in errands or do jobs. In this example, Mother acknowledged her daughter's legitimate feelings about not wanting to go, but asserted the parental right to make the decision.

'Spare the rod and spoil the child' was a popular child-rearing maxim for our parents' generation. Often it was interpreted as simply meaning that children should be punished frequently, as if punishment in itself were somehow good for them. We don't believe that, and will discuss punishment later on, in Chapter 7. However, 'spare the rod' can also be interpreted as suggesting parents should set limits and guidelines for children – that is, not letting them do everything they want. We would agree with such an interpretation wholeheartedly. It has been our experience that children really want parents to set guidelines and to define limits of behaviour.

Rewarding 'bad' behaviour, by repeatedly giving in or being permissive, teaches a child to behave badly. Do this for several months – maybe even years – and you have a spoiled child and later, perhaps, a spoiled adult. So parents should feel free to give lots of love and other social rewards. The key is that *such social rewards are not appropriate to all behaviour, but should be given selectively to the behaviour we like and want to encourage in our children.*

Principle 13: Children will not continue to do things (such as jobs at home) just because parents say 'you ought' or 'I told you to'. There must also be some good consequence (reward).

None of us would like to be called a 'miser'. It suggests someone stingy or selfish. But misers are not just the Ebenezer Scrooges who hoard money. Any of us can qualify as a 'social reward miser'. The necessary characteristics are:

1. Rarely show genuine interest in others;
2. Do not laugh with others;
3. Be cynical about what others are doing;
4. Fail to compliment others on their deeds or achievements; and
5. Keep a safe distance from others.

Think of people in your immediate life situation, such as relatives, friends, employers and acquaintances. How many of them in your judgement would qualify as social reward misers? Finally, how good are *you* at giving out social rewards?

Some parents are social reward misers with their children and are not even aware of it. Often they feel that children 'should' do things out of a sense of duty.

"Children should obey their parents, children should keep themselves and their room clean, children should get good school results, children should do their jobs..." All of these are familiar phrases for children. Society has similar ones for adults: adults should pay their taxes, adults should work hard and be productive, adults should obey the speed limit. Yet, many people do not follow these adult 'rules' solely out of a sense of responsibility. How many citizens would pay their taxes on time if the tax-man didn't care? Would all of us go to work and be productive without a wage packet? Would everyone obey speed limits without the police around?

In just the same way with children, many 'shoulds' don't mean much unless there is some kind of reward (or perhaps even punishment) system involved to back them up. Unfortunately, 'shoulds' often imply the threat of punishment if a chore is not completed. Usually parents or children whose lives revolve around 'shoulds' are carrying a degree of fear or guilt. Parents who are social reward misers frequently expect children to do things out of "you should do" backed by a threat of punishment.

Some parents learn to be social reward misers because they themselves were treated that way as children. Our most important training in being parents, as discussed in the last chapter, comes from our own experience of childhood.

If children are misbehaving and parents are becoming increasingly irritated, there may be less and less social rewarding – this is good training for becoming a reward miser! It is very difficult to give social rewards to someone who makes us angry. This builds into a vicious circle because, as we stop using social rewards, the other person (whether child or adult) has less reason to behave in desirable ways – and so things get worse. When we ignore people who are doing things we want, it is likely they will not do those things in the future.

Dad uses himself as a noble example but fails to give any real social rewards to his son. If Donald continues to do his given tasks, it won't be because of Dad!

Scrooge of the social rewards

It is far better to acknowledge that children, like adults, need social rewards to keep doing the things they must do. Eventually a child will mature to a point where self-given rewards (self-congratulations) will become predominant. Still, we all like a pat on the back for doing something which is not particularly pleasant.

Skimpy use of social rewards will probably result in children not wanting to behave as the parents would like, and may increase the use of threats, punishments, and finally bad feelings within the family.

Adults often get caught in 'miser traps'. While growing up, for instance, men get the message that they are supposed to be strong, silent, and somewhat emotionless. This often leads to holding back with social rewards. We hear a common complaint from unhappy wives: 'My husband rarely says anything nice to me. He doesn't tell me he loves me. He hardly touches me unless he wants sex. I get no appreciation for all the work I do.' The husband who believes that his 'manhood'

59

is reflected best in a strong, silent and non-affectionate approach will very likely turn away from both his wife and children.

Another trap affects divorced parents. Mothers often have custody of children while fathers have access rights at weekends. Sometimes such a situation allows the father to make the mother *appear* to be a material and social-reward miser. When the children spend a weekend with him, they are allowed to do everything they like and have all his attention. Then, when they go back home to their mother who has the day-to-day living responsibilities and cannot provide 'instant entertainment' all the time, they see her as 'no fun' and a miser. Such a situation can deepen the wedge between the divorced parents and certainly doesn't help the children either. (In such a case, it is desirable that the divorced mother should express her concern to the children, talk over the situation with her ex-husband, and try to work out a compromise.)

We have already outlined some of the dangers of being a social reward miser and also pointed out that parents who use lots of social rewards with their children for the right behaviour will be more effective as parents. Just having children behave in ways that we like is a tremendous reward for us as parents! In addition to that, parents who give an abundance of social rewards will receive the same from their children.

The whole idea of popularity, of being liked by others, is based upon this fundamental rule: *you get what you give.*

Principle 14: People who give many social rewards to others tend to receive the same in return.

Just as parents socially reward children, children socially reward us as parents: by doing what is asked of them, having a generally cheerful disposition, smiling and laughing, acting excited and happy when they see us, showing affection, and imitating our behaviour – in short, by making us feel needed and loved. The following example shows how this works.

Children socially rewarding Dad

This father uses social rewards with the children, and he is rewarded when he comes home. The children show obvious pleasure by verbal and physical affection, excitement and by attempting to get him into their play activities. The father can't help feeling good about his children and his reception.

As children grow into the teenage years there is often a marked change in their world of social rewards. They have many friends at school, an entire social structure outside the family, and often come to value those outside sources of social rewards more than those at home. Parents often wonder what happened. They feel that their children no longer consider them so important. There may be some truth in this but, if parents give a lot of social rewards (even to teenagers), it is reasonable to expect that teenagers will reciprocate. Teenagers can socially reward parents by showing affection (although perhaps toned-down), having a sense of humour, talking about their lives, showing interest in what their parents are doing, and not treating them as if they were horribly old-fashioned.

Finally, this principle applies not only between parents and children but is true with any two individuals, brother and sister, husband and wife, employer and employee, or friends.

Chapter Seven

With a Minimum of Fear and Discomfort

What can you do with a child who disobeys, or throws temper tantrums, whines, cries or screams? One possibility is to pay no attention to it at all! This applies to any undesirable behaviour which actually can be ignored without harm to the child, other people or property.

Principle 15: One way to eliminate undesirable behaviour is to ignore it consistently and permanently. Never reward it, even with attention.

There are a few bad behaviour situations which cannot be ignored. These include:

Children physically hurting or endangering themselves. We cannot ignore a child putting a screwdriver into an electrical wall socket or wandering into a busy street.

Children physically hurting or endangering others. We're not talking about 'the usual' fights between children but about situations where one child could seriously inflict injury upon another, such as with a stone, hammer, a big stick or even a fist. This also includes children physically assaulting parents. No one should be expected to ignore an angry child kicking your shins.

Children damaging or endangering valuable property. We have to intervene if a child is breaking things like furniture, drawing on the walls, or ruining somebody's clothes.

Undesirable behaviour which is being rewarded by others, not by parents.

The above-mentioned exceptional behaviour clearly requires more from parents than just ignoring. But keep in mind that a great number of the day-to-day child-behaviour problems faced by most families *are* maintained simply by parental social rewards and can be changed or eliminated by use of the ignoring principle. We advocate ignoring whenever

The incurable thirst

The curable thirst – a different approach

possible, because it avoids unpleasantness (unlike the use of punishment) and requires only a simple removal of social rewards. When correctly done, there is no reward *of any kind* for the child's behaviour from the parent. Behaviour not followed by any kind of a reward will eventually stop, as shown in the next examples.

Her mother constantly rewards Jackie with her attention, calling back and forth, and ultimately giving in. Jackie has been *taught* to ask for a drink of water continually because her mother will eventually bring some. Even if she doesn't, her mother is fun to talk to from the bedroom! Her mother may wonder why this goes on night after night. Why do *you* think it continues? What *could* the mother do?

Before going to bed, this mother made sure Ted had a small drink of water. This eliminated the possibility that he was really thirsty. The first time there was a call from the bedroom, his mother responded, *making it clear she will not continue to answer.* This let Ted know that his mother was around. From that point on she ignored all requests, *never* making the mistake of giving in.

If you are going to use this approach, it is important to explain to the child exactly what you are going to do, and then to follow through without fail. This may mean that you will have to ignore irritating calls time after time, and maybe even hundreds of times, before the child understands. In fact, it often happens that troublesome behaviour which is suddenly ignored, increases for a while before it begins to fade. Success requires time and absolute consistency. The easiest mistake to make is to ignore, ignore, and ignore, and then finally to give in. This can only teach the child to try harder and be more persistent next time.

A common reaction is that it is very difficult to ignore objectionable behaviour, and parents feel they shouldn't have to endure it. 'Do you mean that when John throws a temper tantrum, kicking and screaming on the floor I'm supposed to look the other way? I can't ignore that! I'd give him a good smack!' Our answer is, 'Yes, just ignore it.' Why? First, this is behaviour that *can* be ignored even if there are guests in your house. Admittedly, it is not going to be pleasant. But, if it is ignored without further reward, the behaviour will stop in time, without the use of physical punishment. Punishment involves a variety of bad feelings which should be avoided whenever possible. Second, punishment may deliver a 'mixed' message, because it includes attention – a social reward. So 'a good smack' might help to eliminate the tantrums, but it might not. More on punishment later in this chapter.

Extensive research on temper tantrums has shown that ignoring them is the most reliable and effective approach for eliminating such behaviour. Tantrums are nearly always pro-longed *purely* by adult attention, whether that be smacking, screaming, grabbing, or giving in to whatever the child wants. Ignored, it will eventually stop. So, take a deep breath, and give it a try!

When parents use the ignoring principle with children, it is important to note that something additional is also happening – the child is suddenly being put on a *reduced* 'diet' of social rewards. Since parental attention and social rewards are so essential to children's happiness, the parent should be sure there is no actual *reduction in the total number of social rewards*. This can be done by *increasing rewards for desired behaviour.* If the child has been getting a lot of attention for throwing tantrums, any improved behaviour following such ignoring should be richly rewarded. The overall result is that the child's undesirable behaviour stops, good behaviour in-creases, and the overall quantity of adult social rewards is at least equal and may even increase. If the child were to lose many social rewards as its tantrums cease but no other social rewards appear for other better behaviour, the child may try to regain that attention and parental concern through another form of objectionable behaviour. *So don't stop rewarding,* just stop rewarding the behaviour you don't want!

When a child doesn't obey, do you ever feel like playing the role of dictator and shouting something like, 'Get in there and clean your room or you'll get a smack!!!'?

It is no secret to any parent that strong warnings can work. That is, young children may instantly comply to avoid a smack or whatever. We can see many situations which include 'avoidance learning' in our daily lives. For example, we take aspirin for a headache, not because we like its flavour but to give relief from the pain. In fact, most medicine is designed either to prevent or to get rid of discomfort. The billions of pills people consume each year prove this principle.

**Principle 16: It is rewarding to experience
a sense of relief when we avoid or escape
something unpleasant.**

Using warnings to get a room cleaned

Parents often nag, criticise, scold, or warn children to behave. Children wish to avoid these discomforts and will behave – usually just often enough to escape the unpleasantness and thereby reward the parent for nagging, criticising, scolding, or warning! Thus, parents and children accidentally teach each other to behave in ways which they all find unacceptable!

Obviously the father is upset at the cluttered room but expresses his anger towards the child personally. He makes a vague threat of punishment and Susie obeys largely out of fear. The whole situation brings about negative feelings for everybody. Her father would probably now find it difficult to compliment his daughter no matter how good a job she does cleaning up her room. And Susie, still upset, would find it hard to accept a compliment from her father anyway. As directed, the room is being cleaned, but the entire exchange between father and daughter has been coloured with bad feelings. Let's look at another example.

In this case the father may be upset over the room, but

68

Getting a room cleaned – a different approach

instead of directing his anger at Sharon and creating more negative feelings, he focuses his attention on the room, and insists that it be cleaned before she plays any more. The entire situation reflects the fact that 'that room looks bad' rather than 'the child is bad'. As the room is cleaned up, her father is able to compliment Sharon, who can feel good about the compliment. Although this episode is not exactly one of happiness, neither is it filled with anger or fear.

It should be pointed out that Sharon and her father agree on what a 'clean room' really is! Her father may have to be specific in giving directions to her: 'Please put your clothes in the wardrobe.'

Our next examples relate to the universal problem of getting a child to go to bed. In the first one, it is obvious that this 'countdown', similar to the launching of a missile, produced sudden acceleration, but only at the last second when the end of the count was near. Many parents, like Jacqueline's mother, use the countdown technique, and no doubt it works. But it becomes an opportunity to test just how far a parent will go, a sort of fun game for any child! The game may be fine with the parent, but it doesn't take long for children to work out how to use the countdown game as a way of making a parent 'perform'. The problem is that children are actually being taught to mess about and delay, which can anger the parent. Nevertheless it is the parent who has taught the child to delay. Some parents are not consistent in using the countdown. One time they use it, another time they do not. Or a parent may count to ten on one occasion, yet only reach five on another. This can be confusing to a child.

In the next case, her mother told Lisa that bedtime was approaching, then rewarded her verbally and with a kiss for getting into bed. That should help her to get to bed on time in the future. But what happens if she doesn't go?

In our third case (page 72), the mother has reached the point where going to bed is not something to be delayed, debated, or negotiated. She had already told Dorothy to go to bed, the girl disobeyed, and now she must take the con-

Using warnings to get a child into bed

sequences: her mother tells her to go to bed immediately and hurries her along with a *mild* smack on the bottom. Dorothy learns that her mother means what she says.

We do *not* advocate that parents use warnings or threats to get children to obey. Nevertheless, in the real world there are times when parents have to have obedience from their children and may need to give an ultimatum. *If you use an ultimatum, back it up.* Make it clear what is expected, how soon, and what will happen if the child does not comply. Make the consequence immediate. *Never give an ultimatum you cannot or will not carry out!*

Consider this situation: we were at a beach one beautiful day and observed an interesting situation between a mother and her five-year old son. The boy was in the water playing and his mother said, 'Come on, now, it's time to go.' The child looked up, then went back to playing. The mother, obviously annoyed, shouted louder, 'Johnnie, come here right now!' He ignored her. She shouted again, even louder,

Getting a child into bed – the ideal situation

Getting a child into bed – a different approach

'If you don't come here this instant, we're going to leave without you!' She stood there watching him continue to play. 'We're leaving,' she called, then began walking towards the car while looking back at him. He looked at her, smiled, and continued his play. Finally, very angry, she splashed out into the water, grabbed his hand, and dragged him towards the car. What did she do wrong? Consider her ultimatum. Everyone, including the child, knew she was not really going to leave him behind and she was therefore making an empty threat. When the child tested her on her ultimatum, he learned that it was a bluff.

What is most important about using ultimatums is that parents must mean what they say. Then children will eventually see that what parents say will be carried out. Of course, as children grow older, their parents issue fewer ultimatums. Adults do not give each other ultimatums if they want to get along with each other!

One of the notable aspects of the principle of avoidance is that *children* can train their *parents* by using it! It happens often. Let's say that a young boy knows how to do something that really irritates or annoys a parent, such as whining, crying, shouting, or pestering. He wants to buy sweets, so he finds his father and starts whining. He whines, and whines, and whines. Finally, his father gets angry. What happens next is crucial. His father can ignore him, physically punish him, send him to his room, or – you guessed it! – give him the money. 'Will you get out of here and stop nagging at me?' his father says while handing him some change. The boy leaves and his father sighs to himself, 'That child is going to drive me mad.' He may be right! Look carefully at what just

A missed message

happened: the child whined and whined, and what was the result? He was given money for sweets. His whining was rewarded; it got results! The father escaped from something unpleasant (he got rid of the whining) so he was rewarded too. *Both* have been rewarded, one by getting something nice, the other by getting rid of something unpleasant.

We can predict that the child will continue to whine (and perhaps become a master at it), while his father might give in to his whines even faster. They are caught in a vicious circle, and it was all accidental.

Many people successfully get others to do things by annoying them. Children do it with tantrums, tears, whimpers, destructive acts, pouts ('I hate you'), and a thousand other antics. Adults do it to each other by nagging, ignoring, withholding love or sex, insulting, threatening violence, and in other ways.

Remember: try to keep threats to a minimum. If you feel you must give an ultimatum, make the consequences clear and back it up. Finally, be sure the communication is clear. Stop to think about what you are saying!

Principle 17: Punishment is a way of stopping behaviour which simply cannot be ignored. If punishment is to be used, it must be clearly related to the behaviour, given immediately, of low to moderate intensity, and certain to occur.

Punishment influences behaviour, and fast! That's why it has been around as long as humanity and will probably continue to be around in the future. Punishment is defined as applying an unpleasant consequence (either social or physical) following bad behaviour. But it's a bit like nuclear power: while having great strength, it also has its dangers. For example, punishment used alone does not teach new and correct behaviour, nor does it build positive feelings between people. You cannot separate pain, either physical or social, from the person who administers it. And because punishment does not teach what behaviour is desired, it is crucial that a parent shows or demonstrates what *is* the appropriate way to behave. It is not enough to assume that children do know the right way of doing things when being punished for misbehaviour. *Show them, tell them, guide them towards the right way.*

Punishment – an exaggerated example

Admittedly, this is a tongue-in-cheek example, but the principle still applies. The mother sidestepped her responsibility for administering punishment on the spot and saved it for the father later. He is then greeted at the door with unpleasant family business (to him this is like being punished for coming home). Dinner-time, which should be a family's pleasant and relaxing time together, becomes a situation filled with unpleasant feelings. Also his father called John a 'bad boy', a very negative label and not very specific. What he meant was that Mother and Father didn't like what he did. Consider the difference between 'I don't like *what you did,* it makes me angry,' and 'I don't like *you,* you make me angry.'

In the illustration overleaf, punishment was immediate but calm; it was related to what Jimmy had done, and the amount of punishment seems about right. We believe that parents

75

Using punishment – a different approach

should tell each other when they have disciplined a child. In this case, the father supported the mother's decision, which is essential, especially because he wasn't even there when the event happened. Nor was the father confronted with bad news as he walked into the house. As a result, dinner-time can be free for pleasant kinds of family interaction.

Aunt Martha's home, since she does not usually have youngsters around, has not been 'child-proofed'. It has fascinating and breakable things sitting around within easy reach. Ideally, she would have a few toys for visiting children to play with, but since she doesn't, it is the mother's prime responsibility to keep Stevie from messing with such things – perhaps by bringing toys with her. His mother's verbal commands having had no effect, the only consequence of the breakage is that eventually she makes the child sit with her. From Stevie's point of view, disobeying his mother has resulted in personal attention and getting to sit on her lap, which is a treat. Mother, Aunt Martha, and even Stevie feel more comfortable with Stevie contained on his mother's lap.

76

Punishment – an ineffective approach

However, what the mother has unintentionally done is to reward Stevie for misbehaving!

Many parents, when feeling uncomfortable about what their child is doing, will try to stop the behaviour by holding or cuddling the child. It does stop the behaviour for the moment but, in the long run, it teaches the child that misbehaviour can lead to loving and cuddling. The misbehaviour probably will continue in other situations similar to visiting Aunt Martha's.

In our second example overleaf, his mother identified the

Punishment – a different approach

undesirable behaviour and intervened quickly. She did not reward Larry in any way other than the minimal attention necessary for the appropriate punishment. Nor did she allow the episode to upset talking with her aunt.

'Time Out' is an alternative to physical punishment which allows a parent at home to intervene and stop unacceptable behaviour without threats, hitting, or pain. It means 'time out from rewards', either social or material. It is a little like 'standing in the corner', but with some added features. To use Time Out:

1. *Select a boring place.* Pick a room or closed-off place within a room that can be made free of anything interesting or dangerous to the child. This might be a utility room (with all dangerous articles removed) or another bedroom. It should be lit and not scary (don't use a bathroom or shower cubicle). It must be boring to the child. Never use the child's own bedroom since that is usually full of interesting things. 'Go to your room', for most children, is no real time out from rewards.

2. *Keep the time short.* The idea is to place the child in Time Out, thus stopping the unacceptable behaviour, and then to release the child after about five minutes of quiet and calm. The child should be told 'That's bad behaviour. Go to Time Out.' If he or she refuses, quietly and firmly take the child there. Once in Time Out, the child is told that after five minutes of *quiet,* Time Out will be over. The five minutes starts from the beginning of calm and quiet. The child learns through this process that quiet will be rewarded.

3. *Do not talk.* The door should be closed and there should be no verbal exchange between parent and child. If the door is opened by the child, that means another minute in Time Out. The parent decides when the time is up.

4. *Do not debate.* Don't smack, don't argue, don't get into an argument. Time Out must mean Time Out.

The Time Out approach has been found to be very effective in dealing with troublesome behaviour. It avoids the problems associated with physical punishment and also keeps rewards to a minimum. *It should be used with caution, neither scaring nor hurting the child in the process.* Once again, 'loving firmness' is the rule.

We cannot encourage parents in the use of threats, intimidation, fear, physical or social punishment to get children to behave. There are entirely too many undesirable side-effects and there are also better methods, as illustrated in our other principles. Punishment has its place by *temporarily* stopping behaviour that simply cannot be tolerated or ignored. It also gives parents a chance to teach a more appropriate behaviour immediately once the disruptive behaviour has stopped. But punishment, if used excessively, can only hurt both parent and child, and sour the relationship. It should be kept in mind only as a less desirable method of behaviour change. The methods in order of preference are:

1. Reward the behaviour you like.
2. Ignore behaviour you do not like.
3. Give verbal warnings that will be backed up.
4. Put the child in Time Out.
5. Punish.

It should be clear by now that the most desirable behaviour-change approaches are the first two, because only those avoid significant bad feelings between parents and children.

Why is punishment so popular among parents if it is actually the least desirable method of behavioural change? The answer is that the person doing the punishment *gets rewarded* by the abrupt halt in the disliked behaviour. Remember, when we do things that help us escape or avoid unpleasantness, we will tend to do them again. In short, the punisher is rewarded by punishing. Also punishment is easy, it takes no planning. Unfortunately, some parents become quickly oriented to only giving punishment.

Chapter Eight

Catch Them Being Good

Listen to a young mother's complaint: 'But there's nothing I can reward, he's always naughty!' Consider her statement carefully. Is there really a child who does *nothing* deserving of a social reward? Is any child *always* naughty? No. There is behaviour that this mother can reward, but she just isn't aware of it, or perhaps chooses to ignore it. To be fair to her child and to herself, she must switch to a positive focus, starting actively to look for and reward good behaviour.

A classroom experiment demonstrates our next principle impressively: a student is selected and asked to leave the room. The class then picks a simple action for that person to carry out in the room, such as setting up the chalk board or picking up a pencil rubber. The volunteer is called back into the room and told that he or she is to do something simple and not embarrassing, and that the way to find out what to do is to move around the room and listen to feedback from the instructor. In one situation the volunteer gets feedback in the form of a verbal 'Wrong!' spoken for every move or action in the incorrect direction. In the other situation the volunteer is given a verbal 'Right!' every time a move or action in the correct direction is made.

We can now compare the effects of focusing upon the wrong or right behaviour. The difference is striking. The student being told 'Wrong!' wanders around confused, stopping, starting, and stopping again, rarely reaching the goal except after considerable time. Even if the goal is reached, students who experience this role say they feel upset, stupid, and really embarrassed. In contrast, students given the positive feedback move consistently towards the goal, usually get there rapidly, and feel good about the performance. Which approach sounds better?

Principle 18: It is preferable that parents have a 'positive focus', actively looking for good behaviour in their children and rewarding it.

Examples of desired behaviour which may be rewarded, depending upon the age of the child, might include going to bed, getting up, playing quietly (or noisily, if you prefer!), eating a meal, saying 'thank you', talking with adults, doing

A negative focus on homework

homework (even partially), learning a new game/word/skill, reading a magazine/newspaper/book, getting dressed for school, carrying groceries, putting toys away, NOT interrupting an adult conversation, NOT spilling food, NOT teasing brother/sister... the possibilities really are endless!

Compare the next two examples. If you were a parent whose child brought home a paper half right and half wrong, which would you focus on? Admittedly, 50 per cent by most standards is not a very high score, and you would want your child to do much better. The key question then is what approach will be most successful in motivating better performance? In the first example, Mother is not encouraging as she focuses upon how many answers Carolyn got wrong. She not only punished bad work, but also ignored the good work as well. In fact, she punished showing-homework-to-Mother. Carolyn can easily discover that one way out of the homework problem is to not bring schoolwork home!

In the second example, Sean's mother had a positive focus. She rewarded getting five right and gave Sean encouragement

A positive focus on homework

towards doing even better. She recognised his success, limited as it was, and set an expectation of better things to come.

A positive focus is desirable at all stages or places in life, from infancy through to old age: at home, at work, with friends, or in marriage. Remember the basic reward principle: if a type of behaviour is to be repeated, it must be followed by good consequences. In order to give a reward, one must notice the desired behaviour. Without a positive focus, we cannot efficiently use the reward principle.

It is surprising that many parents fail to use positive focusing even in obvious situations. How many parents make a point of rewarding small children who are playing quietly and co-operatively? Indeed, they are more likely to be ignored until some sort of disturbance is heard! How many parents of teenagers make a point of complimenting them when they do something correctly, such as talk on the phone for only ten minutes, study properly, or come home for dinner on time? How many adults ignore their spouse's good cooking or nice appearance, yet make a point of complaining when dissatisfied? The popular term is 'taking things for granted'. We call it 'failure to focus on the positive'.

Upon first exposure to this idea there is often a 'gut reaction' against it. The response may be, 'Why should I have to reward somebody for doing something they should be doing anyway?' 'Why should I reward my child for work which is not up to standard?' Well, then, consider the alternatives and their effects. If we ignore the behaviour we like, it may stop. If we punish performance that does not match up to our standards, we are also punishing whatever effort went into it. Even if it is hard at times to use a positive focus, and you may have to work hard at doing it, the effects are predictable, positive, and ultimately to the benefit of everyone concerned.

Failure to use a positive focus with others, does something to you. You may become the kind of person who always looks for the bad in people and ignores the good, a prime target for such labels as 'sourpuss', and 'grumbler'. Nobody wants somebody around who is always moaning, nitpicking, and cutting away at others. Remember, we get what we give. A grump will notice that the world is filled with other grumps!

A Brief Review

Let us take a look at what we have discussed up to this point:

1. Most human behaviour is learned, not inherited, and is the result of influences from the world around us. We tend to do those things which are rewarded and to stop doing those things which are ignored or punished. We will have good and bad feelings connected with people and events, depending on whether they are associated with good or bad feelings in the past.

2. Parents have a great influence on children because of the importance of social rewards, and even a glance from a mother or father can be a strong social reward. It is important to keep in mind that children are individuals too, and rewards must be personal to each child.

3. There is no danger of spoiling anybody by giving him or her too many social rewards – unless they are given for undesirable behaviour. We all like to feel good, and if we give out lots of social rewards to others, we will receive them in return.

4. Nobody loves a miser!

Sometimes children do things we don't like and, while the *easiest* way to deal with it may be by punishing, we suggest that you: first ignore it while rewarding some other desired behaviour; then give a clear verbal warning; then try 'Time Out'; and *only* if those don't work should you resort to punishment.

All of this leads to a consistent way of relating to people, with a 'positive focus'. *Look for the things you like and reward them* – that is the best way to guarantee they will continue in the future!

Chapter Nine

Self~esteem is Worth Working for

A recent comment from a frustrated mother went: 'My daughter is always messing around with things, doesn't heed me, and is really getting on my nerves.' We have all heard comments like this from parents, which tell us only that the parent is concerned about the child's behaviour. There is not enough information here to know specifically what the child is doing, nor to suggest any possible remedy.

> **Principle 19: To change behaviour, it is first necessary to 'pinpoint' – that is identify – the behaviour in question so that it can be both observed and counted.**

This frustrated mother said the child is 'messing around with things'. What does that mean? *What* does the child actually *do? When, where,* and *how often?* The mother might reply, 'Well, she opens cupboards and drawers without asking.' Better. Now, *which* cupboards and drawers and what does she do when she opens them? 'Just yesterday she took the clothes out of my chest of drawers and piled them on the floor.' Good! *Now,* we have pinpointed the behaviour so that we can work with it. We cannot deal with 'messing around with', because it's too vague. But we can *observe* and *count* how often a child opens a drawer and empties the contents. Only by knowing how often this behaviour occurs can you expect to change it.

The beleaguered mother also told us that her daughter 'doesn't heed me'. What does the girl *do* that leads to this conclusion? Her mother answers, 'When I ask her to do something she just doesn't do it.' We still need an example of what might be requested, and of the daughter's response. Mother says, 'One example I can think of is, I asked her politely to clean up her room. She said she would, but didn't do it.' We must also determine if this was true of other requests, such as 'helping with the dishes' or 'going to bed'. The mother then becomes even more specific about the 'problem area' requests. We can then determine *specifically* which requests are routinely ignored. Only at that point have we pinpointed the behaviour 'doesn't care', and can begin to change it.

Some examples of specific behaviour that can be observed and counted are: hanging up clothes in the wardrobe; being dressed and ready for school at 7:30; saying 'No'; using swear words (specified); finishing eating meals (all or specified amounts); time on piano practice; crying; interrupting conversations; taking out rubbish; hitting another person; saying 'thank you'. Once parents have specifically pinpointed behaviour, *then* they can begin to bring about change.

It is simple to test yourself on the use of this principle. Think of child behaviour that you like and want to encourage or one which you find annoying. Put down in writing what you would call it and how to identify it. Now, ask yourself three questions: Can I see it? Can I assess it? Could another person using my description also see and assess it exactly as I would? If the answer to any of these questions is 'no', the behaviour has not been pinpointed. We'll discuss assessing and record keeping in more detail in Chapter 12.

Remember the times when you were amazed by some of the tricks performed by animals on TV or at an amusement park? A porpoise jumps through a hoop, a killer whale gives somebody a piggyback ride, or Lassie plays hurt. These performances were taught by trainers who are very familiar with one of the most basic of learning principles, one which applies to animals and humans alike.

Principle 20: Learning a new form of behaviour is a step-by-step process. Generally, the smaller the steps, the easier the learning.

To apply this principle:

1. Divide into small consecutive steps the pinpointed behaviour you want to teach.

2. Teach each step, through description, imitation (modelling) where necessary, and liberal rewards for success at each step.

3. Once a step has been mastered, ask the child to practise it with all the other steps leading up to it, continually reviewing the entire sequence from the beginning.

Teaching a young child to make a bed – an ineffective approach

*Using the step-by-step approach
in teaching a child to make a bed*

4. Proceed step-by-step until the entire behaviour sequence has been mastered. A large success follows many small successes!

Consider the ineffective approach in the last two examples. Mother asked Keith to start making his own bed without first demonstrating exactly what the steps are. She mistakenly assumed he knew how to do it because he had seen her do it. Keith does what he thinks is a satisfactory job and waits for Mother. But she says (by her words, posture, expression, and tone of voice) that he didn't quite come up to expectation. She gave no encouragement for the work he did and she fell into the trap of doing it herself (unfortunately Keith learns that his mother will probably do his work for him if he does it poorly)! She also failed to give him a small step that he could successfully accomplish. Keith still has not learned any of the steps involved, nor has he experienced any real success in what he did.

Kim's mother asked him to do only a small and easy part of a total learning task. She showed how it was done and

90

Getting a child to do homework – an ineffective approach

ask him to imitate her behaviour. She also rewarded him with her touch, a big smile, and praise. Finally she let Kim know what he will learn tomorrow. It may be that she will have to repeat the first steps a number of times before he is fully successful. At this point Kim has worked at the first steps in bed-making and probably experienced a feeling of success in the process.

Let us look at another pair of situations. Michael apparently has no set study time. After dinner he is allowed to become interested in a television programme and then is told to do his homework. This makes homework even more unpleasant than it would be normally, and puts his mother in the position of being like a keeper. Michael stays in his room for half an hour, which is a substantial effort if he actually spent it on homework, but is treated by his mother as if nothing had been accomplished. Instead of rewarding the half-hour of work and allowing a 'break' from study, she actually punishes the child's efforts by sending him back to the bedroom.

Unfortunately, the entire situation has been unpleasant. Homework for Michael probably is a genuine pain. He has been taught merely to stay in his bedroom, not necessarily to study, and studying has been associated with missing television. To make matters worse, because other members of the family enjoy themselves while he doesn't, the entire homework-television situation can only seem unfair to him.

In the second situation, there is a defined time to study. Mother socially rewards Ian with praise and touch after a short interval of study. She also checks his work (to be sure he is actually working), arranges for a short break after half an hour, and at the end of the evening rewards his efforts with praise and a television programme of his choice. This situation has a pleasant outcome, even though 'studying' itself may be unpleasant for Ian.

A footnote concerning study habits: children usually enjoy watching television. Parents can arrange study schedules so that weekly programmes become rewards for study time. In this way studying does not mean missing favourite shows, but serves to earn time to watch those shows. Such times may vary from day to day, but should be planned ahead of time. Activities that children enjoy can be used as rewards for other tasks they need to do but do not particularly enjoy. The example of Ian involved television, but it can apply to telephone use, radios, records, outings, or whatever.

We find that, for practical reasons, the bedroom is usually the place used by children for study. This presents a problem as children mainly sleep and play in bedrooms. Therefore most of the 'cues' in the bedroom suggest something other than doing homework, which hardly helps to maintain a mood

92

Getting a child to do homework – a different approach

for studying! Many students tell us that they get sleepy while stretched out on their beds studying, which is hardly surprising! For effective study, there should ideally be a separate comfortable place, well lit and free from distractions, where only studying occurs. We recognise that such ideal conditions are not always possible. The main idea is that the study area itself should serve as a *cue* for studying, just as a kitchen serves as a cue for eating! Helping your child to find or create a 'study-only' area will be a major step towards improving his or her school work!

Chapter Ten

Kids Can't Wait

A father says to his twelve-year old son, 'Tom, how would you like to earn a trip to Europe next summer?'

'Yes, that would be great, Dad!' the boy replies enthusiastically, 'What do I have to do?'

'Just clean your room up, and keep it that way!'

'Right! It's a deal!'

Two weeks pass, and the father notices that Tom's room is just as big a mess as it ever was. What happened?

Most of us, given the choice, prefer our rewards immediately following our actions, rather than having to wait until a later time. This is especially true for young children, who do not understand the concept of time and delayed rewards as adults do. Children think in the 'here-and-now', not in terms of hours, days or weeks later. To a young child awaiting a promised reward, the end of the day or the end of the week may seem 'light years' away. (Remember, a few hours is a much greater percentage of a child's total life than of yours!)

Principle 21: Ideal timing for rewarding a child is immediately following the desired behaviour. The longer the delay between the behaviour and reward, the less the effect upon learning.

As we get older, we are more willing to tolerate delays between our behaviour and rewards, such as monthly salary. The importance of immediate rewards is really not lessened, however, for we still expect some kinds of continuing social reward at work, such as attention, recognition, or verbal praise. The size of the monthly salary is not the most important factor in job satisfaction for most people. Instead, things like a friendly working atmosphere, feelings of self-worth and accomplishment are far more important. Among the beauties of social rewards are that they can be given immediately and there is no end to the supply.

Giving a delayed material reward – an ineffective approach

Giving a delayed material reward – a different approach

With any age it is important to socially reward right away. Hug, smile, compliment! If material rewards are also to be given, it is not always possible to give them immediately. However, one can give some sort of immediate symbolic or 'token' reward such as a gold star, points, or 'happy faces' drawn on paper. These tokens in effect provide 'credit' that can later be cashed in for material rewards, and thus bridge the time gap between behaviour and result.

Mother wants to improve Amy's dressing time in the morning, so she decides to use both *social* and *material* rewards. The night before, she tells her daughter what the material reward will be. Amy does get ready on time, is socially rewarded, but then discovers that the material reward will not be given until later. That afternoon may be a very long time away for a four-year old and, by the time Amy gets it, the material reward may not relate to getting dressed on time.

Jenny's mother did not want to give toys during the morning rush before school. Instead, she rewarded Jenny both *socially*, with verbal praise, touch, and smile, and *materially*, with the gold star. The child may enjoy touching, seeing, and pasting up the star herself. Later it will be redeemed for a toy. Such tokens are like money or small gift certificates: they don't have any real value alone, but can be cashed in for something desirable. It is essential, of course, that her mother carries out her promise and cashes in the star *that afternoon.*

Sonya's father decided to use a much-dreamed-of material reward to motivate his daughter to do much better at school. Indeed, Sonya may do better at school and earn the new bicycle. However, there are some potential problems here. He has not set out just what higher marks mean, nor what Sonya must do in order to bring up her marks. There is no effort to keep a record and to reward steps leading to better results. Also, the one big material reward is a long time away. There is nothing wrong with giving a bicycle for better marks if that is acceptable to both parents. It is, however, a little like working six months for one big salary payment!

Giving the 'big reward' – an ineffective approach

In the second example, instead of just promising a bicycle for better results, Julie's father pinpointed the behaviour that will count as improvement, and proposed a plan to work towards that goal, step-by-step. It involves monitoring Julie's behaviour and using points as tokens to give her tangible evidence of progress towards her new bicycle. Of course, they will have to work out the details of such a point system. Julie will be directly responsible for her own progress, and will have immediate and consistent recognition for her ef-

Giving the 'big reward' – a different approach

forts. In addition, the parents are dealing directly with the behaviour involved in mark improvement – that is, studying and daily performance. Material reward systems based solely upon results at the end of term often fail because they do not reward day-to-day efforts.

These examples involve large material rewards (eg, a bicycle) for desired behaviour. We want to reiterate that handing out such rewards alone – particularly if done in a cold manner – will not accomplish what is desired. It is essential that immediate *social* rewards be given for the efforts of children (and adults)! Remember: praise, smiles, touch, and hugs are what *really* count in helping people of all ages to feel loved, respected, and appreciated.

Finally, while it is important to reward *others* immediately, the same applies to *one's own* efforts as well. Often accomplishments can go unnoticed by others, not because they don't care, but because they are busy, preoccupied, or just fail to notice. We have all experienced waiting for somebody to compliment some nice thing we have done, but the compliment never comes. It is easy then to say to yourself, 'Why bother?' Such silent suffering is self-defeating.

When you do something nice that goes unnoticed, you can 'prompt' another person (whether adult or child) into noticing it. It's perfectly acceptable to help people to notice the nice things you have done. If you prepared a special dessert and your children didn't respond or act differently, what could you do? Ask them how they like it! When parents fail to notice something children have done, the youngsters may come and tell Mum and Dad about it.

We need all the social rewards we can get, so when we earn them let's make sure someone notices. It's unrealistic to expect that somebody else will always give us those important rewards without prompting. Children can be taught to prompt and to compliment others as well.

Now, at last, you are ready to *change* a child's behaviour. You have pinpointed the behaviour in question, used a positive focus, broken it down into small steps, and have selected rewards that can be given immediately. It is now essential to be highly alert so the child can be rewarded every time the desired behaviour (or step towards that behaviour) occurs.

You want the child to 'get the message' about the behaviour as quickly as possible. The way to do this is to give the message loudly, clearly, and often. That may mean using a liberal amount of social rewards, token rewards, and even material rewards – anything that clearly communicates your satisfaction and pleasure to the child, and which the child finds rewarding.

Principle 22: There are two basic rules for rewarding: every time and occasionally. It is best to start by rewarding the desired behaviour every time it occurs. Eventually a parent can change to an occasional reward.

Once the new behaviour is happening regularly (over a number of days), a parent can begin to gradually 'thin out' the system of rewards. Certainly you don't expect to follow a child around for weeks or months rewarding good behaviour every time it happens, nor is that needed. For example, if a small boy is being taught to say 'Thank you', at first his mother might prompt him ('Say "Thank you", Johnnie'), and praise him lavishly when he says it. Once he is responding correctly, she can prompt him with 'What do you say, Johnnie?' using praise when he says 'Thank you'. Eventually she can just comment on it every now and then: 'Johnnie, I really like it when you say "Thank you".' Indeed, by this time other people may be smiling and complimenting him, and the behaviour will be maintained by natural rewards for politeness beyond those from parents.

A Word of Caution

When we talk about a change from rewarding every time to an occasional schedule, this does *not* mean a sudden shift from liberal rewarding to almost none. What it means is a *very gradual lessening* to a level of social rewarding which is still enough to be effective. Just 'how much' is a matter of judgement. Keep in mind that too little rewarding means ignoring, and that leads to a possible decline in behaviour. On the other hand, you needn't worry about 'too much'

Changing to occasional rewards – an ineffective approach
rewarding: can you imagine receiving too many hugs and smiles (if they are sincere)?

Hopefully, it is obvious in this discussion that we are not talking only about changing a *child's* behaviour; *parents* must change their behaviour too, in order to modify the reward *system* and set up the conditions necessary for the child to change.

Mother used tokens, material and social rewards to get Lyn ready on time in the morning. Since the girl had managed it well for a week, Mother decided to cut down on the rewards. Her mistake was to cut down much too fast. As a consequence, Lyn has reverted back to being late.

The second mother will gradually cut back on the material rewards, but is maintaining the social and token rewards for Brenda's improvement. The change to a once-a-week reward may involve some negotiation, but most children will remain motivated by pleasing parents if those parents are good social rewarders. Eventually her mother may also phase out the stars and chart, but should never completely stop giving social

Gradually changing to occasional rewards
– a different approach

rewards for getting ready on time.

Many of the things that we do as adults involve mostly self-rewards. We tell ourselves, 'I did a good job on that'. We look with satisfaction at our accomplishments, small or large, and congratulate ourselves, or treat ourselves to something special. This self-rewarding is not 'automatic', but learned. Some learn it well while others do not seem to learn it at all. Self-rewarding is simply having a good opinion of one's own efforts; parents can teach this to children by noticing their accomplishments, and getting the child to point out a job well done and express pride in it. 'Johnnie, you did a great job. You can be proud of yourself. Don't you think so? Tell me about the good job you did.' Ultimately the self-rewarder still needs social rewards from others, but does not always need to depend upon the opinions of others, and values his or her *own* opinion most of all!

Chapter Eleven

Clear Messages

We can only learn to deal with the world around us if we can predict with some degree of accuracy what to expect. It's easy for a parent to be inconsistent. For example, screaming and shouting may be tolerated one day but severely punished the next. Also one parent may approve of certain behaviour while the other frowns upon it. Parents are sometimes inconsistent with different children – one child is allowed to get away with something while another isn't.

Principle 23: It is important that parental approval or disapproval of behaviour be consistent and be made clear to the child.

A good example of inconsistency is shown in the next cartoon, where Mother told Nicole that she couldn't go out until she had finished her dinner. Yet soon after, Mother backed down and allowed the child to go and play after a few bites. This kind of inconsistency teaches Nicole that she really won't have to finish her dinner at all because her mother will eventually change what she said to do. The next night, however, her mother _does_ stick with what she said by carrying out her threat and sending the child to bed for not finishing

Inconsistency with one parent

dinner. Here is a second inconsistency, since one night leaving food on the plate was tolerated while the next night it was punished. From Nicole's point of view, the whole experience seems confusing and unfair.

In the next case, her mother was specific about what should be done, how long Wanda had to do it, and what would happen it she didn't. No further attention was given. She did not have any reminding or prodding, and finally her mother

Consistency with one parent – a better approach

carried out exactly what she said she would do.

Many mealtime problems can be avoided if parents observe two rules:

1. Do not allow children access to snacks near mealtime, and
2. Avoid serving excessive portions of food (especially disliked foods). It is unrealistic to expect a child to 'clean the plate' if it is covered with heaps of food.

In the illustrations on pages 108-109, we have two other examples. In the first case, Barny's mother had a Saturday agreement with Barny that he must mow the lawn so that he could go to the cinema that night. He understood this, yet failed to mow the lawn. His mother kept her part of the bargain in not allowing him to go the cinema. But then Dad 'overruled' her and told Barny he *could* go.

Here we see inconsistency between parents – the failure of one to support the other. Dad, in this case, gets to play the 'good guy' (which automatically makes Mum the 'bad guy'). The result is that his mother is now angry, and Barny has learned that he can get around his parents through 'divide and conquer'. Furthermore, if such inconsistency occurs often, it can put serious strain upon a marriage. Overruling is sometimes used in unhappy marriages as a hostile way for a husband or wife to get at each other. When it occurs for any reason, it undermines parental authority and teaches the child to manipulate adults.

Obviously Dad supported Mum in the next example and made it clear to Scotty that they are united when it comes to dealing with his behaviour. If parents disagree they may wish to discuss the matter privately. Then they can let the child know their joint decision. Neither parent should have the power to 'overrule' the other in front of the child without prior discussion; nor should one parent reluctantly comply, while making the other out to be a villain. For example, the father would have done this had he said to his son, 'It would be fine by me, but your mother has already said no.' This may be consistency, but it is certainly a weak variety.

In our examples, we have demonstrated inconsistency with one parent and between parents. There are, of course, many

Inconsistency between parents

additional variations of inconsistency. For example, a child says to Father, 'Mummy said I can have a bar of chocolate.' In fact his mother has said no such thing. In such cases, a parent who doubts the child's word should always check.

Another common situation involves having different standards of conduct for different children in the family. One child should not be allowed to break 'house rules' while another cannot. No child should get special unearned privileges because of age or sex. (It is, of course, appropriate to allow more mature children certain freedoms which are not yet available to their younger brothers and sisters.) Older children frequently feel angry when younger ones 'get away with murder' because 'they are too young to know better'. Even small children understand basic rules of conduct. A favourite game for older children is to put younger children 'up to something' that will get them into trouble. Consistency in punishment is no virtue if the wrong child is branded the culprit! You cannot, of course, treat each child in the same way. Nevertheless, make every effort to be consistent.

Consistency between parents – a better approach

Finally, think back to our examples involving the lawn and cinema. Let us again assume the son and his mother have an agreement that if he mows the lawn he can go to the cinema that night. Further, suppose that he mows it, does it on time, and does it well. However, later that same afternoon, he does something wrong. His mother becomes very angry, and tells him in no uncertain terms, 'No cinema for you tonight!' In other words, everything is off. She may indeed have reason to be angry and to do something about his misbehaviour; but this issue has nothing at all to do with the lawn-and-cinema agreement! Mum has suddenly, and perhaps unfairly, cancelled the entire agreement after her son has completed his part. The right to go to the cinema was already earned throught his efforts in mowing the lawn. Parents must be willing to carry out their side of the bargain made with their children (just as they would with other adults) if they want to retain their credibility. The mother may want to punish her son, but it should not involve the film.

We understand that it may be difficult for a suddenly-

Rewarding with a mixed message

angered parent to give a child a previously-earned reward. It is very tempting, when angry, to withdraw *all* good things from a child including previously-earned rewards. Yet it is essential in this situation that Mum and Dad 'grin and bear it'. Parents must stick by their agreements if their word is to mean anything.

There are, of course, extreme situations where an agreement may appropriately be changed. For instance, assume the boy had fulfilled the agreement, but later deliberately injured his sister. Should he still be allowed to go out that evening? Most parents would say 'No!' Perhaps a compromise is in order when *serious* misbehaviour occurs. Mother might react to the new situation by modifying the agreement: 'You completed the lawn, and I owe you a trip to the cinema for that. But, you also hurt your sister, so you're not going out *tonight.*'

110

Rewarding without a mixed message

The most common form of combining reward with punishment is in the statement, 'I like that, but...' For example, 'That was a good job, *but* I think you can do better.' 'I like your new hair style, *but* I think I liked it better when it was longer.' 'Your room looks a lot better, *but* your wardrobe is still a mess.'

Principle 24: When parents combine punishment with reward, it is confusing to children. The punishment usually has the greatest impact, leaving the child with predominantly bad feelings.

Because we are all human, *absolute* consistency is not possible. Nevertheless, it is very important to avoid 'changing the rules', father-mother contradictions, and lack of follow-up on agreements. If we expect our children to behave consistently, we need to provide them with good models to follow!

We have set out the importance of having a positive focus and looking for good things to reward in others. It is also essential that when we socially reward someone, we do not add a social punishment at the same time. This is very easy to do, particularly if you are trying to switch from a negative focus to a positive focus.

The 'but...' offsets the value of the reward, leaving at best a rather shallow social reward. Often, it is no reward at all because the person responds emotionally to the negative aspect of the remark. It's like getting a pat on the back and a kick on the bottom at the same time! Compliments and criticisms given together mix about as well as oil and water.

In the examples on pages 110-111, Dad has a choice. He can make a big thing out of the good job the boy did with the dishes (positive focus); he can direct his attention towards the water spilled on the floor (negative focus); or he can respond to both. Certainly Dad does not want the boy to spill water on the floor while rinsing dishes, but that is a separate matter. What counts is that Tom and Jim did rinse the dishes and put them into the dishwasher. Dad should reward the dish cleaning, as in the second example, without any mixed message. Then he can attend to the cleaning-up separately. He can also reward the boy for helping with the cleaning-up.

This principle may seem rather obvious, yet we have found that many people liberally dish out mixed messages while being convinced that they are actually good social rewarders. Good intentions are not sufficient if parents mask punishment in what they consider to be social rewards for their children. It is easy to check yourself as a social rewarder. Take notes (or have someone else take them) and record what you say to others in the way of compliments. See if you add a 'but...' If you discover that you are masking punishment in rewards, we say to you, 'Congratulations for trying to have a positive focus, but...'

Chapter Twelve

Keeping Track

How do you really know whether your attempt to change a child's behaviour is working? Sometimes it's obvious, but often you don't know – *unless* you keep records.

If you have pinpointed behaviour and want to begin changing it, it is best to start with information on *how often* it is happening. Mental records or impressions are not enough, for our memories are notoriously faulty. One of the greatest failures in behaviour-change programmes is not keeping accurate records. Behaviour change can be a slow process and, even though it is actually happening, a parent may not be completely aware of it at the time with only casual observation.

**Principle 25: Before trying to change
behaviour it is helpful to count the number
of times it occurs, usually over a period of
a few days.**

Once you have pinpointed the troublesome behaviour, the following steps should be taken for adequate record keeping:

1. *Redefine (if necessary) the behaviour in a positive focus.* It is typically human to see problems in terms of behaviour we don't like. However that means we are watching and counting undesirable behaviour – a negative focus. Any negative behaviour can be redefined so we can direct our attention towards the positive behaviour that should take its place. For example:

The Problem in Negative Focus:	The Problem in Positive Focus:
Wet pants	Dry pants
Hitting brother	Minutes of co-operative play with brother (no hitting)
Not eating everything on plate	Eating everything on plate (or specified amount)
Late	On time
Interrupting adult conversation	Minutes of not interrupting adult conversation
Bad talk (eg 'You fool')	Good talk (freedom from bad statements)
Excessive telephone conversations (over a specified length)	Reasonable telephone conversations (within a specified length)
Bed left unmade	Bed made

To express behaviour in positive focus is essential because, when we are ready to make a change, we want all our efforts, attention, and concern to be directed towards the *desired* behaviour. That can only happen with a positive focus. Catch them being good!

2. *Design a method of counting the behaviour.* Recall again that it is important to obtain a measure of the behaviour *before* anything is done to change it. At this point parents should continue to behave in their normal way. If you are going to teach toilet training you need to decide how often to check and over how long a period. Just checking one morning or relying upon your memory is not sufficient. Again, with each measure of behaviour,

it is important for the parents to continue to relate to the child exactly as before during the 'counting' period, thereby providing a normal opportunity for the behaviour to occur. For example, if you are checking 'dry pants', don't change your child's fluid intake or start taking him or her to the toilet more often. If observing co-operative play, don't provide a new set of toys to play with. When checking how well your child eats, don't change the types of food served or portions given. If you want to see how often someone is on time, don't change the types of situations involved. To get an idea of how often your child interrupts your conversation, keep your conversation patterns the same, in the usual places and at the usual times.

Some possible methods of counting the positive-focus types of behaviour are given in the table on page 116.

3. *Count the results.* Use a simple sheet and record the behaviour as it happens, keepinng it accurate throughout the specified time. Don't try to trust this job to your memory alone. Do not show it to the child (remember, you are not yet trying to do anything to change the behaviour). Add it up so you have a total for the week or period involved. For example, you might find that your child had dry pants on thirty-two out of seventy occasions (or about 46 per cent of the time). Or there might be fourteen interruptions during the three and a half hours of monitored parental conversations that week (or four per hour). This is the *before* count.

At the end of your attempt to change the child's behaviour you will want to carry out the same checks on the behaviour: for the *after* count. It can then be compared with the *before* count, to decide whether your efforts have been effective. The *before* and *after* behaviour counts will be clearly different if the programme had any effect. If there is no difference, then it's back to the drawing board. Remember, the problem is *not* with you or the child, but with the programme you designed. Try again – and continue to keep accurate records!

Problem in Positive Focus	Method of Counting
Dry pants	Ten checks per day (hourly between 8am and 6pm) for a week
Minutes of co-operative play with brother	While the children are playing, Mum or Dad can observe three 15-minute blocks per day for a week (preferably unnoticed by the children), counting acceptable minutes
Eating everything on plate (or specified amount)	Number of times everything is eaten per 10 meals at home
Punctuality	How often on time, out of 20 opportunities to be either late or on time
Minutes of not interrupting adult conversation	Carry on parental conversation one half-hour per day for a week in front of the child and in the situation they normally interrupt. Count the number of minutes free of interruptions
Good talk (**Important:** concepts such as 'polite talk' must be clearly understood by parent and child to mean the same thing!)	For a week, following each request made of the child, record the response (to tell how often they replied with 'polite talk')
Reasonable telephone conversations	Record the length of **every** phone conversation you are aware of for a week. Note the calls which are longer than the specified time
Bed made	Check every morning over a period of two weeks

Brother and sister 'fights' are a common family experience. However it is not evident in this example just what Wendy wants to change. In her conversation with Mildred. Wendy was not clear about the type of behaviour to which she objected. What exactly is 'fighting'? She did not set up a systematic method of observing the behaviour, relying instead on her impressions. Obviously the children cannot be fighting

116

Brother and sister fighting
– an ineffective plan for behaviour change

'all the time', (although we know it can often seem that way)! After her talk with Mildred, Wendy set up a reward system *not connected to any specific behaviour* (how does she decide which nights to give dessert?) Finally, as she had no accurate *before and after* behaviour count, she did not know whether her effort *really* worked or not. Maybe it worked; but maybe it didn't. She doesn't *know.*

In the example on page 118, Mary has pinpointed a desired behaviour (in a positive focus) by defining it in an observable and countable way. She is measuring how often it occurs *before* attempting to do anything about it. Her friend Jan expresses the feeling of urgency many of us experience when we want to change disruptive behaviour in our children. We want to get it changed immediately and not take time to collect and record information about it. However, Mary wisely is going to take that time and tolerate the behaviour just a little longer. This will serve as a solid basis from which to begin her behavioural change.

117

*Brother and sister fighting
– a different plan for behavioural change*

Keeping careful records of behaviour is hard work and often takes valuable time that could be used for other things. It is tempting and easy to 'ease off' and just try to keep a mental record of behaviour. Unfortunately it rarely, if ever, works. Written records made immediately after the undesirable behaviour occurs *will* tell you whether your efforts to change that behaviour are working, and to what degree. There should be no vague statements like 'maybe it's working' or 'it seems to be helping'. Only after you have pinpointed the behaviour and recorded how often it happens are you ready to set out to change the behaviour effectively.

Chapter Thirteen

The Family that Works Together

Imagine this situation: Mum and Dad have two young children. At the end of the day, Dad comes home, hoping to watch the six o'clock news. The children are running about, making a lot of noise. Dad calls out to Mum in the other room. 'You're at home with these children all the time. Can't you do something about this noise? I work all day and I'd like to come home just once in a while and have a little peace and quiet.' This father believes that it is the mother's responsibility to make sure the children are quiet when he is there.

In a minor variation of the same situation, Mum may come home from work to hear Dad say, 'These children have been a terror today, and I want you to do something about it!' he believes that the mother has responsibility to deal out the punishment and may have threatened the children with 'Just wait until your mother gets home!'

Some parents believe that 'boy problems' are Dad's responsibility while 'girl problems' are Mum's. A mother will say 'Can't you do something with that son of *yours?*' while the father suggests, 'You'd better have a talk with *your* daughter.' Such division of parental responsibility is inefficient for dealing with child problems. We advocate an equal relationship, with shared roles and responsibilities.

Principle 26: All members of the family should be involved in changing a child's behaviour.

A family is built upon a complex system of situations between parents, children and often relatives. It should be apparent that a child's behaviour is unlikely to change if only one family member modifies his or her reactions while the others continue on as before. If we want any behavioural change programme to be effective, it must include all members of the family, specifying the part each person plays in the situation, what they must do, and how they must change. Everybody can be involved in the planning by sitting down together and talking it over, so that everyone knows what is going on.

Consider this dinner scene: Becky needs to lose weight

Cutting calories – ineffective family involvement

and the other family members are certainly involved. The trouble here is that they also suffer by having to miss favourite desserts. No attempt was made to include the family in a positive focus upon better eating habits. In fact, her younger brother takes delight in having a negative focus as he points out his sister's continuing poor eating habit.

In the second example, the eating habits of the other family members are not affected by Betty's diet. They do not suffer because one person has a weight problem. Also, the group is encouraged to help Betty with her eating and not sabotage her efforts. Uneaten food is removed from the table so Betty is less tempted to have second helpings. She is given the choice of staying at the table and watching the others eat chocolate cake or going to another room (which might be less painful if she really wants cake). Finally, Dad makes a point of encouraging her. Her ten-year old younger brother said nothing directly to Betty. This may be the best support one can realistically expect from a younger brother. (If the

Cutting calories – effective family involvement

younger brother did continue to comment on and tease his sister, Mum might want to deal directly with his teasing by making *his* dessert an earned reward for not teasing during dinner.)

Weight loss is a slow process. Pounds do not suddenly disappear, and any person changing their eating habits needs all the encouragement possible. With all family members involved and on a positive focus, there can be lots of social rewards for exercising, eating smaller portions, and giving up high-calorie foods.

Thus, regardless of the behaviour to be changed, you need to be sure that all family members are involved, know how to socially reward the desired behaviour, and follow through. Treat it as a family project where nobody feels excluded. It is particularly important that no family member suffers by a programme to change another's behaviour, because the likely reaction to an undeserved penalty is to sabotage the programme.

How do you get other children in the family to co-operate with a behavioural change programme, rather than ridicule the child involved or sabotage parents' efforts? It's no secret that children enjoy teasing and annoying each other, and may even be delighted when the other one gets into trouble with their parents. In short, children can develop an acute sense of negative focus by eagerly picking away at anything they know will irritate a brother or sister. The end result is that Mum or Dad must play referee. When dealing with a specific behavioural problem, we want to be sure that not only Mum and Dad, but also the brother and/or sister, have a positive focus on the improved behaviour. Reward sharing provides a reason for the other child to encourage a change in behaviour rather than hinder it.

**Principle 27: One way of including members
of the family in changing a child's behaviour
is through reward sharing: everybody
experiences something nice as a result of the
child's success.**

Choosing the reward to share must be done carefully. It has to be something that everybody likes and it must be special – that is, something which doesn't occur very often. In other words, *it is not already a regular part of family entertainment.* If it's routine to go out for a meal every Friday night, don't suddenly insist that one child has to behave correctly or nobody goes out. That puts everybody in the position of being punished if the child in question does not immediately perform well. It may result in great pressure from brothers or sisters who don't want to be cheated out of their normal fun. Once the special family reward has been selected, behaviour is then recorded and socially rewarded, step-by-step. Possibly points or stars can be used until a desired goal is reached. Then the family can share the special reward.

The emphasis is not on *if* the goal is going to be reached, but *when.* Parents should also avoid planning shared rewards that are *time limited,* running out at a certain date and placing a child under pressure ('If James gets 50 points *by Sunday,* we can all go to the beach'). Instead, it should be planned to allow the child to achieve success at his or her own pace (*'When* James has collected 50 points, we can all have a day at the beach').

In the first example, Dad set up a shared reward for the boys and specified the behaviour required, but expected a perfect record by the next weekend. When Wayne carried out his task for three out of five days, he got no reward for his partial success. Dick was completely faithful to the task, yet he too got no reward. Dad set it up so that any failure on Wayne's part would automatically result in punishment for both boys, regardless of how well Dick did his job. Conflict between the two boys can certainly be expected.

David's Dad, in the second example, sets up a shared reward system for both boys. No one is left out, and both are earning points towards separate family goals. Dad has set no time limit, so he rewards *any* improvement in David's efforts. The boys know that eventually they will be going to a cricket match. Also Joel is likely to show more interest in David's success and may even remind him to take care of his pet. Remember, in a good reward sharing plan, you must be sure that the children are sharing rewards and not being

Taking care of pets – ineffective reward sharing

punished through denial of an expected reward. Keep in mind that rewards are a personal thing. With children of very different ages, you may have to do some searching for a reward that interests *everybody!* It is certainly desirable to ask, and to discuss with the children, which rewards would make everybody happy.

Besides being helpful in changing one child's behaviour, there are also broader family benefits of reward sharing.

124

Taking care of pets – effective reward sharing

There is a shift toward a more positive focus and away from a 'failure' orientation. In addition, such joint efforts tend to give the family a sense of unity through working together.

Chapter Fourteen

The Spice of Life

Almost everybody likes to be told 'I love you' by someone special. However, if that is said 100 times a day, it is going to lose meaning and value. Similarly, a child may consider raisins to be a favourite treat, yet they would cease to be of interest if Mum gives out a pound of them during the course of a day! Parents should keep in mind a wide variety of possible rewards to use with their children.

Principle 28: All children like variety.
Nobody enjoys the same thing all the time.
Some rewards can be used so much that
their effectiveness is lost.

Some of the more popular rewards are listed in the following table. You can add to the list for a specific child.

One of the reasons token rewards are so useful with children is that they allow for so much variety. Money, clearly 'material', is also really the most valued 'token' of all! For adults or children, it can be exchanged for any of the desired material things in life. Likewise points, game chips or stars can be cashed in for various children's rewards.

When trying to get some additional reward variety in day-

Social Rewards	Token Rewards	Material Rewards	Activities
Attention	Stars	Sweets or biscuits	Cycling
Winks	Points	Raisins	Cinema
Looks of surprise or joy	Drawings of happy faces	Crisps	Going to swings
Smiles	Marks	Ice cream	Picnicking
Verbal praise	Game chips	Small toys	Swimming
Hugs	Cards	Clothes	TV time
Kisses	Play money	Games	Special privileges
Affectionate touch	Money	Money	

to-day activities, one approach for parents (perhaps an obvious one) is simply to *ask* children what kinds of things they enjoy or would like to earn. It may happen that older children will say, 'Oh, I don't know, I can't think of anything.' Parents can get around this seemingly disinterested attitude by carefully observing their children and noting what kinds of things they spend their spare time doing. You can assume these are things they enjoy. Write down these activities and then allow children to earn *time* for them: for example, if a son spends a lot of time watching TV, use that time as a reward for studying. If a daughter enjoys bicycle riding, let her earn time for her rides on her bike. If a child is excited about shopping on Saturday with the weekly pocket money, let that money be earned by correctly doing daily tasks. Keep in mind a child's wide variety of favourite activities. You can make those activities dependent upon desired behaviour.

A question often raised on this approach is, 'Isn't this a little like tricking the child – making an activity they already like into a new reward?' Nothing is secret or hidden in this approach. Everything is to be clearly explained to the child. The only thing new is in requiring that behaviour be reward-related. The alternative is for the child to engage in all the enjoyed activities *without* doing necessary tasks (or whatever behaviour is involved), and then have his or her parents nag and perhaps even punish. That approach is not likely to win any prizes for effectiveness! It's far better for a child to do tasks *first,* and *then* earn the right to engage in enjoyed activities – free of parental nagging or punishment. Making rewards dependent upon desired behaviour teaches a child responsibility – a valuable lesson for later life.

We have all had the experience of being 'burned' because a verbal agreement is later remembered very differently by the people involved. Memories being notoriously faulty, adult agreements or transactions often require written documents. Similarly child-adult agreements within the home can be 'spelled out' in writing.

**Principle 29: Parents and children can form
a contract, written or pictorial, that
specifies the desired behaviour and the
rewards concerned.**

The purpose of a contract is to provide an agreement which clearly specifies the behaviour expected and the rewards that can be earned. It is written in simple language (or pictures for small children), is displayed publicly, and helps the parties involved remember the terms of the agreement. Often such an agreement is posted somewhere in easy view and can be used for recording daily behaviour change, such as earning gold stars or points. With young children, parents usually set up a contract on the basis of what they already know about rewards for their children. With older children, parents may need to negotiate a contract – that is, specifying what they want the children to do, exploring what the children would like to earn, and agreeing upon a fair system of behaviour and rewards.

Parents may have to spend considerable time with the children in negotiation because of disagreements about the value of rewards (children sometimes are unrealistic about the cost of material things), and the amount of effort that should go into earning them. Like management and labour, parents and children can usually reach an agreement and can finally 'sign' the document to show good faith. If the terms of the contract are carried out by the child, parents must follow through on their end of the bargain. If either party cannot abide by the agreement, the contract should be terminated and a new one drawn up. It is usually best to make a contract for only a short period of time (a week or two), since experience may find it to be too easy or too difficult.

Even the best contracts have to be reassessed every now and then. Having a written contract is valuable because it requires a positive focus, serves as a visual reminder of the agreement, and keeps both parents and children on target.

In carrying out such a contract, Mother may wish to check the room with Sally in the afternoon just before her daily snack time. She already knows Sally likes biscuits, chocolate milkshake and fruit. Yet, it may be necessary to prompt Sally at first, re-explain and show her how to do each of the things

A contract for a young child

shown in the pictorial contract, using the step-by-step principle. After a couple of days, Sally should be able to manage
without further instruction, depending on her age and physical skills (and upon the degree of perfection her mother
expects)!

A number of assumptions are included in this example of
a contract. First, the child must know exactly what the tasks
involve (when defined as 'bed made' or 'table cleared'). Second, the parents will have to decide which are the more
important aspects of behaviour to them and which seem to
be the easiest. Points are then weighted accordingly. We are

BEHAVIOUR	TIME CHECKED	POINTS POSSIBLE	POINTS EARNED						
			MON.	TUE.	WED.	THU.	FRI.	SAT.	SUN.
FEED DOG, FRESH WATER	8 AM	1							
BED MADE	8 AM	1							
HAIR COMBED	TWICE A DAY	2							
TABLE CLEARED	8 PM	2							
RUBBISH TAKEN OUT	8 PM	2							
EVENING HOURS FREE OF INSULTS TO SISTER	HOURLY 6 TO 10	4							
	DAILY TOTAL								
		WEEKLY TOTAL							

REWARD COSTS	POINTS
FILM (FAMILY)	40
ROLLER SKATE (FAMILY)	40
OUT FOR PIZZA	40
HAVING FRIEND OVERNIGHT	20
MAKE A DESSERT	20
CHOICE OF TV PROGRAMMES FOR ONE EVENING	10

SPECIAL REWARD
WHEN A TOTAL OF 150 POINTS
HAVE BEEN EARNED,
YOU CAN HAVE A PARTY.

_____   _____
SIGNED (PARENT)   SIGNED (SON)

A contract for an older child

131

also assuming that the sister who is being 'insulted' is able to focus positively and determine, on an hourly basis, whether she was insulted or not. (The *problem behaviour* is 'insults', which are easy to count, but that would be negative focus. The sister must be able to record time *without* such insults so that the family may reward it.)

In the sample contract, the child gets a choice of how to cash in earned points. There is a long-term 'special reward' included so that, after 150 total points are earned, a party can be given. Such events happen occasionally in most families anyway, so why not include a party for a special reward? The chart shows daily progress and steps towards the big reward. If the child is doing a good job on most items, the parents may allow self-monitoring (or self scoring) and marking-up of points (with occasional checks for accuracy). The whole thing finishes about three week later (an older child may be able to handle this longer period), and may be reassessed at that time if necessary.

Remember, in forming a contract:
1. Pinpoint the desired behaviour.
2. Whenever appropriate, state the checking time when the improvement in behaviour has to be completed. Just saying 'feed the dog daily' could mean any time within 24 hours.
3. State the behaviour with a positive focus.
4. Clearly specify what the rewards are, their cost, and when they will be given.
5. Place the contract in a public place for all to see. Most children really like earning things and seeing their progress publicly displayed.
6. Re-evaluate the contract on a weekly basis to determine effectiveness. If necessary, new reward values can be assigned to desired behaviour. For example, if an improvement in behaviour is not occurring at all, the reward may be too small and can be increased.

Contracts are a common means of adult communication. They require both parties to be clear about their desires and expectations, and they specify both rewards for successful completion and penalties for failure. If we are to improve our communication with children, such clear statements can be of great value. Although a written contract is not always necessary (just as it is not always necessary between adults) it does allow for fewer misunderstandings. Also, a written contract says to both parties' 'We are serious about changing things here!'

Chapter Fifteen

Relax, Nobody's Perfect!

A young mother was recently in our office describing what it is like to be divorced, working full-time, and trying to bring up three children (aged 3, 7, and 9). She looked haggard as she sighed, 'I've tried everything I know – yes, even behaviour modification, but that didn't work. The children are at each other, fighting and screaming, answering me back, and I don't have a moment's peace.' She began to cry, then described in more detail the constant turmoil in her home. Her own efforts went unappreciated, and a great deal of friction among all of them made each day unhappy.

This mother had a tremendous responsibility and felt she couldn't keep on functioning without some freedom from chaos at home. She said she had 'tried behaviour modification' so we probed further. She had made an effort but not a very efficient one. It seems she had devised a reward system

---

Principle 30: Considerable time and effort are needed for behavioural change. Each of us has spent a lifetime learning to become the way we are. You shouldn't expect people to change overnight.

---

based upon a negative focus and had failed to include any step-by-step planning. Furthermore, she had given her effort at changing things only one week to succeed. When nothing changed, she gave up.

The young mother described above needed help in obtaining accurate behaviour counts and in making a number of revisions in her behavioural change programme. We encouraged her to try again, but this time she was urged to carry on with it for at least a month. She reported back to us each week on how it was going. Her summary reports:

First week: Not much difference.

Second week: The only marked change is that John isn't screaming so much. He talks in a normal voice more often.

Third week: The two oldest children are getting on better. There has definitely been less fighting.

Fourth week: Maybe this approach is going to work after all! Four of the six desired behaviours have really changed. There's a better atmosphere at home.

Changing a single small behavioural problem in one person can be quite a task. Imagine the complexity of problems this mother had to deal with!

It is only natural to want fast results in dealing with troublesome behaviour but that desire must not stop us from working realistically. Recall the ignoring principle (see Chapter 7). Just as you may have to ignore undesirable behaviour repeatedly, so you may have to pay careful attention and lavishly reward behaviour you like hundreds of times before you consider it completely satisfactory. You may need to experiment, revise and change contracts, juggle points around, rephrase wording, and renegotiate with older children. As we have stated before, all this is hard work for any parent and can test your patience when there is no dramatic change overnight. Our advice is to carry on with it for at least a month, once you think you have a good programme. If it's still not working – remember, it's not the *child's fault*. It's not *your fault*. It's a *faulty programme!* That means back to the drawing board and some more thought.

It's a reality of life that as children get older, they fall more and more under the influence of social reward systems outside the home and family. Their friends, their school and their activities may command much more of their interest than do parents, family or events at home. This means that parents have less and less direct effect upon their children's behaviour. As children grow up it is no longer easy to restrict access to prized rewards and choose the appropriate behaviour to earn them. Sometimes parents experience these changes with a feeling of helplessness, worrying about their children and then blaming themselves if the children get into trouble ('Where did I go wrong?'). A parent cannot feel responsible for everything a child does because there are other strong influences upon any child's behaviour. Also a parent cannot expect to have as much effect upon a maturing teenager as upon a five-year old!

Parents may have to watch teenagers grow away from them somewhat and do many things which they dislike. Also they may be unable to do much about it! The boys' hair length struggle of the 1960s/1970s is a classic example. A teenage boy may be far more influenced by the social rewards from his friends and girlfriends than by the approval of Mum or Dad. If his girlfriend likes long hair, that is probably what the boy will wear. When parents see that their approval and social rewards have lost some influence, they sometimes attempt to use coercion with teenagers and become bogged down in power struggles. In the long run such struggles cannot improve the family relationship, and may poison the later establishment of a rewarding adult-to-adult relationship between parents and their growing children.

Parents *can* relate positively with children approaching adulthood and not feel guilty by assuming that everything the child does is their 'fault'. With adulthood, most children will come to a new appreciation for their parents' company, interest and approval, but on an adult-to-adult basis.

Throughout this book we have tried to make clear that being a parent is hard work and a great responsibility. With consistent effort and positive involvement it can also be a joyful experience. These thirty behavioural principles, when systematically used, can produce major improvements in family life, both for parents and children. Parents are happy when their children succeed and can be praised. Children are happiest when parents are pleased with them – smiling, hugging and laughing, rather than frowning, nagging and punishing.

Don't get discouraged if you find yourself having difficulty applying these principles consistently. All of us are human and nobody is perfect! No one can expect to do 'the right thing' all the time. Even if some 'all-knowing' psychologist were to lay down the ABSOLUTE RULES showing how one should bring up children to be PERFECT, no human being (including the psychologist) could follow them all the time!

We hope this book has been interesting and helpful to you. Our thirty principles, although not new or 'revolutionary', do suggest a turnabout in some of the ways that parents often relate to children.

Our message is both simple and complex. Each person's sense of well being, enjoyment of the good life and self-worth, all depend upon understanding and gaining some control over the consquences of his or her actions. This is as true for parents as it is for children.

We are actually talking about lifestyle, a way of relating to children *and* adults, in which we look for the good things in ourselves and others, and purposely develop them. People grow when we socially reward often, ignore what we don't like, and punish sparingly if at all. Do remember that people don't change instantly! We all need encouragement as we improve little by little. Such a lifestyle includes consistency instead of chaos, a focus on today rather than tomorrow or yesterday, and an active sharing with others of a world rich in variety and warm relationships.

The benefits go far beyond the immediate improvement in behaviour. Children who are brought up with a positive focus and lots of social rewards learn to relate to others in the same way. Their friendships during the developing years will be enhanced, and their adult intimate relations and perhaps interactions with children of their own will be based upon this positive approach. They also learn to reward themselves and to be successful in achieving their own goals. There is no better definition of self-sufficiency and happiness!

A LIST OF THE THIRTY PRINCIPLES
USED IN THIS BOOK

1. Labels – such as 'hyperactive', 'aggressive' or 'insecure' – really don't explain behaviour, nor do they give parents guidance in how to deal with their children.

2. Behaviour is influenced by two major factors: heredity and learning.

3. Most human behaviour is learned. Children learn both desirable and undesirable behaviour in the same way.

4. All people, including children, behave differently depending on where they are and who they are with.

5. We keep doing things which bring good results or good feelings (rewards).

6. We stop doing things which bring bad results or feelings (no rewards).

7. Our learning experiences determine when we feel such natural emotions as love, elation, anxiety, and sadness.

8. Because each person is unique, rewards must also be unique – that is, 'tailor-made' to fit the individual.

9. We all like material rewards such as money, food or toys. But it is really social rewards like attention, praise and affection that make us feel good about ourselves.

10. Attention is one of the most powerful social rewards, for both desirable and undesirable behaviour. Even scolding a child is paying attention and may be rewarding!

11. Much of our behaviour is learned by imitating the people around us, particularly parents.

12. Parents need not worry about giving 'too much' love and

affection. The way to 'spoil' a child is to reward undesirable behaviour.

13. Children will not continue to do things (such as jobs at home) just because parents say 'you ought' or 'I told you to'. There must also be some good consequence (reward).

14. People who give many social rewards to others tend to receive the same in return.

15. One way to eliminate undesirable behaviour is to ignore it consistently and permanently. Never reward it, even with attention.

16. It is rewarding to experience a sense of relief when we avoid or escape something unpleasant.

17. Punishment is a way of stopping undesirable behaviour which simply cannot be ignored. If punishment is to be used, it must be clearly related to the behaviour, given immediately, of low to moderate intensity, and certain to occur.

18. It is preferable that parents have a 'positive focus', actively looking for good behaviour in their children and rewarding it.

19. To change behaviour, it is first necessary to 'pinpoint' – that is, identify – the behaviour in question so that it can be observed and counted.

20. Learning a new form of behaviour is a step-by-step process. Generally, the smaller the steps, the easier the learning.

21. Ideal timing for rewarding a child is immediately following the desired behaviour. The longer the delay between behaviour and reward, the less the effect upon learning.

22. There are two basic rules for rewarding: every time and

occasionally. It is best to start by rewarding the desired behaviour every time it occurs. Eventually a parent can change to an occasional reward.

23. It is important that parental approval or disapproval of bad behaviour be consistent and be made clear to the child.

24. When parents combine punishment with a reward, it is confusing to children. The punishment usually has the greatest impact, leaving the child with predominantly bad feelings.

25. Before trying to change behaviour, it is helpful to count the number of times it occurs, usually over a period of a few days.

26. All members of the family should be involved in changing a child's behaviour.

27. One way of including members of the family in changing a child's behaviour is through reward sharing: everybody experiences something nice as a result of the child's success.

28. All children like variety. Nobody enjoys the same thing all the time. Some rewards can be used so much that their effectiveness is lost.

29. Parents and children can form a contract, written or pictorial, that specifies the desired behaviour and the rewards concerned.

30. Considerable time and effort are needed for behavioural change. Each of us has spent a lifetime learning to become the way we are. You shouldn't expect people to change overnight.

CHECKLIST FOR A BEHAVIOURAL CHANGE PROGRAMME

1. Identify the behaviour. Ideally work with one or two relatively simple ones rather than a whole set.

2. Define the behaviour (pinpoint) so that it can be *observed* and *counted.*

3. Rephrase any definition from a negative focus to a positive one.

4. Observe and count the behaviour as it happens without changing anything. Do this for at least a week.

5. Devise a system of rewards that are most likely to work for that person – especially social rewards.

6. Explain the plan to the child and other family members.

7. Implement the plan, be consistent, reward immediately, and use a variety of rewards.

8. Shape the behaviour by rewarding step-by-step progress towards the final goal.

9. Keep the programme going for a pre-determined period of time, measured in weeks, not days.

10. Keep checking the behaviour and note progress. Revise your plan if necessary.

Index

142

Other useful books from Exley Publications

Your Guide to Better Sex, £9.95. A helpful guide book for any couple experiencing sexual problems. The author is one of the world's leading sex therapists, who studied with Masters and Johnson, and this 300-page book is packed with the latest medical research and case histories.

It Worked for Me, £3.99, (pb). Over 1,000 practical tips for coping with young children including dealing with tantrums, crying and sleeplessness, child-proofing the home, medical and other emergencies, and ways to encourage self-esteem in children. A useful book for all parents with young children, and an attractive gift.

Feeding your Child, £3.99, (pb). Sound, practical advice on the correct feeding of babies and young children, as well as pregnant mums. The author is a nutritionist and a mother. A useful book for parents and health visitors.

Help! I've got a Teenager! £3.99, (pb). A very helpful book for parents tearing their hair out because of their teenagers. The authors are psychologists and joint parents. They offer step-by-step advice on such problems as what to do if your teenager won't clean his or her room, is failing at school or is sexually promiscuous.

Choices: a teenage girl's practical workbook for career and personal planning, £9.99, (pb). A book that every mother, grandmother, aunt and mentor will want to give to the 'teenage' women in their lives. It's beautiful, but pre-eminently teaches young girls to be independent and self-reliant.

Challenges: a teenage boy's practical workbook for career and personal planning, £9.99, (pb). The companion book to *Choices* now brings practical help and guidance to boys in making life's vital decisions and acquiring the necessary life-skills.

Is There Life After Housework? £3.99, (pb). A revolutionary book which sets out to show how you can save up to 75 per cent of the time you spend on cleaning. It is written by Don Aslett, a millionaire who heads one of the largest cleaning firms in the world. Humorous illustrations throughout. It's a natural gift for the hardpressed and downtrodden!

How to Win at Housework, £3.99, (pb). Don Aslett's first book was such a success that he soon had a vast fan mail from readers asking him how to solve their particular cleaning problems for them. He decided to write a second book dealing with the hundred most commonly asked questions:– 'Do I dust or vacuum first?' – 'Is there an easy way to clean venetian blinds?' – 'How do I get rid of pet pongs?' He brings to this book his long experience, sensible advice and lively sense of humour.

The Secret of Freedom from Clutter, £3.99 (pb). Save your sanity – not your cardboard boxes, souvenirs and old shoes – and Don Aslett shows you how insidious clutter really is. It not only crowds out cellars and attics, it blunts our effectiveness as people. With a hilarious 'Junkee's identity test', he helps you assess just how bad your problem is; he lists the hundred and one feeble excuses for hanging on to clutter and gives you hundreds of practical ideas for getting rid of clutter.

Who Says It's a Woman's Job to Clean? £3.99, (pb). A provocative – yet highly practical – handbook for men. Dare you give this to the man in your life – or to your sons? Written by a man who is now a millionaire because he became a professional cleaner, this will show even the most unliberated male how to transform daily living and make everybody happier. This book is fun, practical and essential reading for men – however the publishers take no responsibility for the divorce rate....

Free colour catalogue available on request. Books may be ordered through your bookshop, or by post from Exley Publications Ltd, Dept BD, 16 Chalk Hill, Watford, Herts, United Kingdom WD1 4BN. Please add £1.00 per book for postage and packing.

Exley Publications reserves the right to show new retail prices on books, which may differ from those previously advertised.